Sue Hackman | Alan Howe | Patrick Sco

Hodder Starters: English
WORD LEVEL

Hodder & Stoughton

A MEMBER OF THE HODDER HEADLINE GROUP

ACKNOWLEDGEMENTS

The author and publishers would like to thank the following contributors:

Maria Moran	• Sections	A Vowels
		B Plurals
Judith Langley and Nisha Tank	• Section	C Suffixes
Sue Haigue	• Sections	D Prefixes
		E Roots
		F Apostrophe
		G Homophones
John Williams	• Sections	H Unusual word families
		I Learning Strategies
Sonya Austin	• Sections	J Vocabulary
		K Link words
		L Language variation

Orders: please contact Bookpoint Ltd, 130 Milton Park, Abingdon, Oxon OX14 4SB. Telephone: (44) 01235 827720, Fax: (44) 01235 400454.
Lines are open from 9.00am - 6.00pm, Monday to Saturday, with a 24 hour message answering service.
Email address: orders@bookpoint.co.uk

British Library Cataloguing in Publication Data
A catalogue record for this title is available from The British Library

ISBN 0 340 79072 5

First published 2001
Impression number   10 9 8 7 6 5 4 3 2 1
Year   2005 2004 2003 2002 2001

Cover photo © Randy Faris/Corbis.
Typeset by Lorraine Inglis.
Printed in Great Britain for Hodder & Stoughton Educational, a division of Hodder Headline Plc, 338 Euston Road, London NW1 3BH by Hobbs the Printers, Totton, Hampshire.

Contents

KS3 English Framework objectives

This grid shows which KS3 English Framework Objectives for Year 7 are covered in each starter activity.

STARTER ACTIVITY	KS3 OBJECTIVES (YEAR 7)
A. Vowels	
1. Long A 1	Wd 1 Vowel choices
2. Long A 2	Wd 1 Vowel choices
3. Long E	Wd 1 Vowel choices
4. Long I	Wd 1 Vowel choices
5. Long O	Wd 1 Vowel choices
6. Long U	Wd 1 Vowel choices
7. OW and OU	Wd 1 Vowel choices
8. OY and OI	Wd 1 Vowel choices
9. AIR, ERE, EAR, ARE and EIR	Wd 1 Vowel choices
10. AW and AU	Wd 1 Vowel choices
11. OOR and ORE	Wd 1 Vowel choices
12. EI and IE	Wd 1 Vowel choices
13. Vowels and double consonants	Wd 1 Vowel choices
14. Softening C	Wd 1 Vowel choices
15. Softening G	Wd 1 Vowel choices
16. Quiet consonants	Wd11 Strategies for learning spelling
17. Hard-to-hear vowels 1	Wd 1 Vowel choices
	Wd 11 Strategies for learning spelling
18. Hard-to-hear vowels 2	Wd 1 Vowel choices
	Wd 11 Strategies for learning spelling
19. Revision	Wd 1 Vowel choices
	Wd 11 Strategies for learning spelling
B. Plurals	
1. ES plurals	Wd 2 Pluralisation
2. Plurals for words ending in Y	Wd 2 Pluralisation
3. Plurals for words ending in F	Wd 2 Pluralisation
4. Plurals for words ending in vowels	Wd 2 Pluralisation
5. Unusual plurals	Wd 2 Pluralisation
6. Revision	Wd 2 Pluralisation
C. Suffixes	
1. Suffixes which change the grammatical function 1	Wd 3 Word endings
	Wd 19 Lexical patterns
2. Suffixes which change the grammatical function 2	Wd 3 Word endings
	Wd 19 Lexical patterns
3. Occupations 1	Wd 3 Word endings
4. Occupations 1	Wd 3 Word endings
5. SHUN endings 1	Wd 3 Word endings
6. SHUN endings 2	Wd 3 Word endings
7. Consonant suffixes	Wd 3 Word endings

STARTER ACTIVITY	KS3 OBJECTIVES (YEAR 7)
8. Vowel suffixes	Wd 3 Word endings
9. Compounding full, all and till	Wd 3 Word endings
10. Losing E	Wd 3 Word endings
11. Modifying words ending in Y	Wd 2 Pluralisation
	Wd 3 Word endings
12. Able or ible 1	Wd 3 Word endings
13. Able and ible 2	Wd 3 Word endings
14. Sede, seed, sede and ceed	Wd 3 Word endings
15. IC endings	Wd 3 Word endings
16. Changing letters	Wd 3 Word endings
17. L endings 1	Wd 3 Word endings
18. L endings 2	Wd 3 Word endings

D. Prefixes

1. Adding prefixes	Wd 4 Prefixes
2. Prefix loop game	Wd 4 Prefixes
3. Number prefixes	Wd 4 Prefixes
4. Latin prefixes	Wd 4 Prefixes
5. Common antonyms	Wd 4 Prefixes

E. Roots

1. Root words	Wd 10 Analogy Wd 16 Unfamiliar words
2. More word webs	Wd 10 Analogy Wd 16 Unfamiliar words
3. Common roots	Wd 10 Analogy Wd 16 Unfamiliar words
4. The spelling of roots	Wd 10 Analogy Wd 16 Unfamiliar words

F. Apostrophe

1. The omissive apostrophe	Wd 6 Apostrophes
2. The possessive apostrophe	Wd 6 Apostrophes
3. Its and it's	Wd 6 Apostrophes
4. Possessive plurals	Wd 6 Apostrophes

G. Homophones

1. Homophones	Wd 5 High-frequency words
2. Two, too and to	Wd 5 High-frequency words
3. Common homophones	Wd 5 High-frequency words

H. Unusual word families

1. Ough and ought	Wd 10 Analogy
2. Eigh and eight	Wd 10 Analogy
3. Unusual consonant digraphs 1	Wd 10 Analogy
4. Unusual consonant digraphs 2	Wd 10 Analogy

I. Learning strategies

1. Creating acronyms	Wd 11 Strategies for learning spellings
2. Referring to related words	Wd 10 Analogy
	Wd 16 Unfamiliar words

STARTER ACTIVITY	KS3 OBJECTIVES (YEAR 7)
3. Words within words	Wd 10 Analogy
	Wd 11 Strategies for learning spellings
4. Mnemonics	Wd 11 Strategies for learning spellings
5. Learning by sight	Wd 11 Strategies for learning spellings
6. Learning by sound	Wd 9 Phonemes and syllables
7. Looking it up	Wd 12 Using a dictionary
	Wd 15 Dictionary and thesaurus

J. Vocabulary

1. Working out words you don't know	Wd 16 Unfamiliar words
2. Terms of qualification	Wd 18 Qualification and comparison
3. Terms of comparison	Wd 18 Qualification and comparison
4. Less or fewer?	Wd 18 Qualification and comparison

K. Link words

1. Words for comparing and contrasting	Wd 20 Connectives
	Sn 13f Discursive writing
	Wr10 Organise texts appropriately
2. Temporal connectives	Wd 20 Connectives
	Sn 13b Recount
	Sn 13d Instructions
3. Causal connectives	Wd 20 Connectives
	Sn13c Explanation
	Wr 12 Develop logic
4. Connectives for adding and summating	Wd 20 Connectives
	Sn 13c Explanation
	Sn 13e Persuasion
	Sn 13f Discursive writing
5. Words for use in argument 1	Wd 20 Connectives
	Sn 13e Persuasion
	Wr 15 Express a view
6. Words for use in argument 2	Wd 20 Connectives
	Sn 13e Persuasion
	Wr 15 Express a view
7. Prompt words for creative thinking	Wd 20 Connectives
	S&L 12 Exploratory talk

L. Language variation

1. Words borrowed from other languages	Wd 22 Words in different languages
2. Words with close relatives in other languages	Wd 22 Words in different Languages
3. American vocabulary and spelling	Wd 22 Words in different languages
4. Changing language	Wd 22 Words in different languages
5. Meanings and context	Wd 14 Word meaning in context
6. Definitions	Wd 14 Word meaning in context
	Wd 15 Dictionary and thesaurus

Introduction

About starters

Like all the best ideas, starters are nothing new. Effective teachers have always known that a fast and focused start creates a positive atmosphere for learning, and gets the lesson off to a flying start. Starters give a sense of quick gains early in the lesson and this builds pupils' confidence. They also help to break the lesson into manageable spans, so that attention can be caught, developed and then re-captured with a shift of focus.

Typically, a starter might last around 10-15 minutes depending on the length of the whole lesson, and focus on one idea. Its speed and focus lends itself to 'spotlighting' key ideas or conventions, and thus to direct teaching.

Active learning

Starters are not a passive learning experience. That would undermine the idea of an engaging start. Most of the starters are posed as problem-solving activities or investigations, and pupils are drawn in to investigate and solve the challenges posed by the starters. All of the starters are organised as whole class activities, and there is a high premium on oral, interactive and participatory work. Most of them feature short bursts of work in pairs or groups, particularly where investigative thinking is required. Pupils are expected to consider what they already know and generalise from it. The idea is to spark off thinking by drawing out latent knowledge for exploration.

Teaching starters

Starters do not claim to be exhaustive teaching, even though they are explicit in nature. It is for the teacher to apply and secure them in practice. In reading lessons, attention can be drawn to words that have recently been covered. Vocabulary starters are particularly well-placed against lessons spotlighting different types of writing. It is in shared writing, however, that spelling starters find their application. Vowel choices, for example, are hardly a problem in reading, but they are the crunch issue for most secondary spellers. The teacher can pause to ask the class how to make the right choice, and recapitulate conventions covered in the starters. In other words, the starter launches the teaching of spelling, and guarantees coverage, but share writing is where the learning is secured.

The pace of teaching is cracking. Starters depend on focus and challenge. At first, teachers over-run because the prevailing teaching style in secondary schools is geared to exposition and immediate contextualisation. Starters operate on a slightly different (but not mutually exclusive) premise that you can teach explicitly and rapidly and then consolidate in two ways: firstly, by revisiting 'little and often', and secondly by highlighting the techniques studied when the class reads and writes longer text.

The benefit of doing it this way is that it allows you to deal with skills, conventions and techniques in passing with a lightness of touch when you teach reading and writing. We do a disservice to literature if we try to spin off it every aspects of language teaching: it can be both spurious and frustrating for the reader. And anyway, we can't be sure that all the things we need to teach will be covered if we wait for naturally-occurring opportunities.

The content of starter sessions

The use of starters ensures the systematic coverage of objectives, and releases us from ruining texts by having to teach these things from first principles every time we come across them.

The starters address the word-level objectives in the Framework of Objectives for English in Year 7. If the pupils have been taught the National Literacy Strategy in Year 6, they may well have come across some of the terms and ideas.

Issues

Resourcing

Providing the ideas and resources for intensive short-burst starters is the aim of this book. It provides step-by-step teaching plans and OHT masters for almost a hundred starters. A number of starters also include photocopy word cards or sheets when an investigation is too large to fit on an OHT. It is probably worth the effort of laminating the cards to keep for further use.

Another valuable resource is a collection of hand-held mini-whiteboards so that pupils can have a go at the spellings taught, and show you their attempts immediately. They love the impermanence of the whiteboard: it holds no threats. Cheap and compact whiteboards can be created by laminating A4 white card.

Differentiation

Starters work well with the less able because they are engaging and short and also because they yield clear learning points. The able like them for much the same reasons: they see them as challenging, pressurised and explicit. Most starters work well in a mixed ability setting, but there is absolutely no point in doing a starter if the pupils already have the rule or topic under control.

There are built-in supports for differentiation in a typical starter activity, because a typical sequence poses incremental challenges:

► Identifying patterns – the vast majority of pupils should be able to do this
► Generalising about patterns – the majority of pupils should be able to do this
► Explaining patterns and conventions – many pupils will be able to do this
► Finding and rationalising exceptions – some pupils will be able to do this
► Extending or speculating about a pattern – a few pupils will be able to do this

The challenge lies in the pressure to articulate and to explain, and then to apply effectively.

Managing answers

Since starters are interactive and direct, there is a premium on the ability to manage discussion. The whole-class approach means that one has to be quite careful to create a climate in which mistakes are tolerated and construed as learning opportunities.

There is a tricky moment when you receive an incorrect answer. You want to value the effort but you also want to remedy the misconception. In general, it is best to tackle misconceptions as a whole class matter, and not to single out the pupil who made the error. The problem can be avoided if the starter is treated as a short investigation for which a range of solutions can be suggested and then tested. At least one good reason for doing it this way is that it mirrors the real-life working process of clever thinkers.

Never dodge. If it's wrong, say so, but follow up with a constructive comment: 'but I can see why you thought that'; 'but you took a sensible approach'.

Assessment

Starters offer instant assessment. You get immediate feedback on the success of your teaching, and you don't store up time-consuming marking. A classroom assistant can be well used at the front of the class, noting the responses of pupils, and perhaps returning to the topic later with a smaller group.

Fun

It is hardly fashionable to say so, but starters are also good because they are fun. Boys in particular warm to the oral and direct approach. And if they are not fun, the worst they can be is brief and businesslike. It is not dreary to be direct: it can make life easier. But don't wait to be persuaded: try them and see. Starters will sell themselves to you because they work.

Sue Hackman

A1 Long A (1)

YOU WILL NEED:

▶ OHT A1.1

▶ Two colours of highlighter pen

1 Show the top half OHT A1.1 and ask pupils to compare the vowel sound in each column. Look for the difference between long and short A.

2 Ask pupils how they could describe the sound of the long A. Look for the answer that the vowel says its own name.

3 Reveal the rest of the OHT and ask for a volunteer to come out and pick out in one colour, three words containing long A. Next ask for someone to pick out in another colour, three words containing short A. Alternate until all the words have been identified.

apple	**essay**	**blame**	human
Santa	**main**	cat	jacket
carrot	rabbit	band	**baby**
face	stand	**pain**	match
vein	**rain**	**rein**	**reign**
act	**sail**	**ale**	**play**
stay	anchor	ant	bank
track	**pray**		

(Long vowels in bold)

4 Remove the OHT and ask pupils to tell you the four different ways of making long A that appear on the OHT, with an example. They should find:

A-E (as in hate)   AY (as in pray)

AI (as in pain)   EI (as in vein)

5 Ask if anyone can think of words making long A with any other letters e.g.

A in acorn

EA in great

EY in they

Remind pupils that these versions apply to only a small number of words.

A2 Long A (2)

YOU WILL NEED:

▶ Cards A2.1, enough for one set between two

▶ OHT A2.2

▶ Three colours of highlighter pen, enough for one set between two

1 Remind pupils of the main ways of making long A from the last starter, and explain that today you are going to focus on choosing the right alternative between the three main choices: A-E, AI and AY.

2 Distribute to pairs the sets of cards made from Handout A2.1 and ask pupils to sort them into three columns for A-E, AI and AY.

3 Put up the questions on OHT A2.2 and allow pupils 5 minutes to consider their responses. After the first minute, tell pupils they need to consider the position of the sound in the word. After two minutes, tell them to consider the letter that follows the sound.

4 After 5 minutes, take feedback. Look for the following answers to the questions:

1 What is the most common way of making the long A sound?

A-E

2 AY usually appears where?

At the end of words

3 How to do you choose between A-E and AI?

A-E is much more common.

Look at the following letter. If it is D, L, M or N it could be either. All the rest are usually A-E. There <u>are</u> exceptions, but they are not in frequent use.

A3 Long E

YOU WILL NEED:

▶ OHT A3.1

1 Show the top part of OHT A3.1 and show pupils that long E can be described in much the same terms as long A: we call it a long vowel if it says its own name. Use the two lists to exemplify this.

2 Show the middle section and ask pupils to pick out, very quickly, the four words containing long E: feet, delete, reason, conceive.

3 Now show the table in the bottom section of the OHT and ask pupils to work in pairs to list three words which make a long E sound using each of these alternative digraphs, trying to find one example at the beginning of a word, one at the middle and one at the end.

Beware answers which contain the letters but not the sound. This is a listening exercise.

Sample answer:

	Beginning	**Middle**	**End**
ee	eel	feet	decree
ea	each	bean	sea
ei	either	ceiling	-
e-e	even	scene	-
ie	-	thief	-
other	era	demon	-

A4 Long I

1 Explain to pupils that long I is made in much the same way as long A and long E – the vowel says its own name as in the words 'bright', 'lie', and 'eiderdown'.

2 Challenge pupils in small groups to come up with as many ways as they can of spelling the long I sound in words, providing three examples of each way. For example:

> **IGH**
> thigh
> bright
> sight

3 After three minutes, take feedback. Sample answers:

IGH	thigh, bright, sight
IE	lie, flies,
I-E	white, wine, prize
Y-E	type, hyper, tyre
I – other vowel	icon, virus, iron
Y – other vowel	dynamic, pylon, dynamite
End Y	try, imply, apply
EI	either, eiderdown, height

4 Ask pupils which they think it the most common. Look for the answer: I-E. In fact, the split diagraph is the most common vowel choice across all the vowels. The rest need to be learnt.

5 It is useful to learn the common strings such as -ind, dyn- and -ight. Note that there are a huge number of long I curiosities, for example 'eye' and several -ind words ('mind', 'rind', 'wind', etc).

A5 Long O

YOU WILL NEED:

▶ Dictionaries

1 Given their experience of recent starters, ask pupils to suggest what the long O sound would sound like, and get them to suggest words containing it e.g. 'bold', 'rose', 'boast', etc.

2 Now ask pupils in groups to brainstorm words containing the long O sound with spellings they are sure of, or they may use a dictionary. Allow 2 minutes.

3 Ask them to come up with the three most common ways of making the long O sound. Look for the answer: OA, O-E, OW.

4 Ask them which is the most common. Look for the answer: O-E. Remind pupils that the split diagraph is the most common long vowel spelling across the vowels.

5 Ask them which one to choose if the sound is at the end of a word. Look for the answer: OW (e.g. 'show', 'grow', 'know', 'throw').

6 Ask pupils to spend 1 minute thinking of any word which uses long O but doesn't involve the letter O. (e.g. 'sew', 'plateau', 'gateau')

7 Ask pupils to brainstorm words ending in O (e.g. 'trio', 'concerto', 'piano', 'halo', 'tomato') and identify patterns. A large number, for example, are musical terms imported from the Italian language in which the O ending is very common.

A6 Long U

1 Given their experience of recent starters, ask pupils to suggest what the long U sound would sound like, and get them to suggest words containing it e.g. 'flute', 'root', 'fruit', etc.

2 Tell pupils that there are many different ways of representing the long U sound in spelling. Challenge them, in groups of 3 or 4, to come up with as many as they can, with examples. Allow 3 minutes.

3 Look for:

U-E (as in 'tube')

U – (as in other vowel 'uniform')

UI (as in 'fruit')

EU (as in 'feudal')

UE (as in 'glue')

EW (as in 'flew')

OO (as in 'root')

OU (as in 'soup')

Infrequent examples:
OE (as in 'canoe')
End U (as in 'emu')

4 Ask pupils which is the most common spelling. Look for the answer: U-E and remind pupils that the split digraph is the most common choice across all the vowels.

5 Ask pupils to identify which four of the eight common spellings can't appear at the end of words. Look for the response: the first four (U-E, U- other vowel, UT and EU) can't be used at the end; the others can, e.g. 'rescue', 'blew', 'taboo', 'caribou'.

6 Ask pupils to brainstorm words beginning with each vowel spelling, to identify any words which can't begin with them. For example:

U-E	'use'
U–vowel	'university'
UI	-
EU	'eulogy' and several proper nouns e.g. 'Euston'
UE	-
EW	only proper nouns e.g. 'Ewbank'
OO	rare and colloquial e.g. 'oodles', 'oomph'
OU	usually pronounced as in 'ouch' when used at the start of words.

A7 OW and OU

YOU WILL NEED:

1 Explain to pupils that there can be confusion about choosing between OW and OU when you make the /ow/ sound as in 'shower' and 'mouth'. It is made more tricky because both OW and OU have a range of other possible sounds ('scour', 'pour', 'though' and 'flow', 'flower')

2 Ask pupils if they can think of a third way of making the /ow/ sound. Look for the answer: OUGH as in 'plough'.

3 Write up three key words on the board:
SHOWER   SOUR   PLOUGH
Then say the following words aloud and ask the pupils to allocate them to the lists on the board. Build up lists.

drown

shout

(continued overleaf)

hour

vowel

growl

couch

sound

crowd

blouse

drought

drown

Next, a homophone:

bough (of a tree)

bow (curtsey)

Next:

aloud (spoken)

allowed (permitted) (point out the -ed indicating past tense)

Draw out the -ed for past tense and the way OW appears at the end and OU in the middle of words. 'Allow' in this case is the base word ending in OW to which -ed has been added.

A8 OY and OI

YOU WILL NEED

▶ OHT A8.1

▶ OY and OI cards made from A8.2, enough for one pair each

1 Show OHT A8.1 and give pupils a couple of minutes in pairs or threes to look for patterns and come up with guidelines for choosing OY or OI.

2 After 2 minutes, take suggestions and reward good attempts to find patterns. Look for the following responses:

- OI is the most common choice at the beginning or middle of a word
- OY is the most common choice at the end of a word
- OY is therefore the most common choice when the word carries a suffix.

The last point is important. Words that end in OY can be extended by suffixes. Pupils need to attend to the base word to be sure of the right vowel choice.

3 Distribute the OY and OI cards made from A8.2 so each pupil has both. Read aloud the list opposite and ask pupils to raise the correct choice for each word. You can see at a glance which pupils have got the right answer and which need reinforcement.

enjoy

boisterous

alloy

cloister

rejoice

enjoyment (enjoy + ment)

decoy

embroidery

destroyed (destroy + ed)

employer (employ + er)

4 Draw attention to 'voyage', 'royal' and 'loyal'. The Y in these words is used to avoid having three adjacent vowels.

A9 AIR, ARE, EAR, ERE and EIR

YOU WILL NEED:
▶ OHT A9.1

1 Show OHT A9.1 but keep the columns EAR, ERE and EIR covered. Explain that AIR and ARE can represent the same sound, and illustrate this by writing in the top line: 'chair' and 'glare'.

2 Ask them to spell and position the following words, provided orally:

beware

prepare

repair

despair

Write them in.

3 Now point out how many words ending in this sound are homophones. Go through this list and ask pupils to differentiate the spellings and meanings:

hair/hare

fair/fare

stair/stare

Write them in.

4 Now reveal the other three columns and explain that here are three more ways of spelling the same sound.

5 Present more homophones, again asking pupils to differentiate the spellings and meanings:

where/wear   pair/pear/pare

their/there   bear/bare

6 Ask pupils how they remember the difference between homophones. Take suggestions and offer:

- PEAR – shares key letters with EAT – Eat a pear.
- THERE shares key letters with HERE and WHERE – a sense of place in common.

7 Allow a moment for pupils to suggest similar ways of 'fixing' a homophone by relating it to another word.

8 Ask pupils to brainstorm other words using the same sound.

9 Draw out which are the most common choices (AIR and ARE).

A10 AW and AU

YOU WILL NEED:

▶ Cards A10.1, enough for one set between two or three

1 Use the words 'Autumn' and 'claw' to illustrate the two main ways of spelling the /au/ sound.

2 Distribute the sets of cards and ask pupils to sort the words into groups depending on the position of the sound in the word i.e. beginning, middle or end.

3 Ask pupils to generalise about the relationship between position and spelling.

4 Take suggestions from the class and look for the following responses:

- Endings are usually AW, but watch out for words where suffixes have been added e.g. 'drawer'
- In the middle position, AW usually comes before an N or an L e.g. 'lawn', 'shawl'.
- AU can be used at the beginning or middle of words.

5 Draw out exceptions: 'haul', 'awful', 'awkward', 'awesome'.

A11 OOR and ORE

1 Write up the words 'door' and 'core', and point out that OOR and ORE represent the same sound.

2 Give pupils 2 minutes in threes or fours to brainstorm two lists of words ending in OOR or ORE.

3 After 2 minutes, ask pupils which is the most common way of spelling the sound. Look for the answer: ORE. Take a moment to check the OOR list, to be sure that pupils know the high frequency words 'poor', 'door, 'floor', 'moor'and, 'spoor'.

4 Now challenge pupils to take 1 minute to come up with two other ways of spelling the same sound, with examples. Look for the following:

OUR (as in 'pour')

AUR (as in 'aura', 'centaur')

5 Now challenge pupils to brainstorm homophones and their meanings for the following words which you can deliver orally, then draw/spell on the board:

1 spoor - animal's trail (n)
   spore – seeds (n)

2 poor – opposite of rich (adj)
   pour – empty (v)
   pore – tiny openings in skin (n), read with intense concentration (v)

3 moor – hill (n), secure a ship (v)
   more – extra (adj)

4 boor – person without manners (n)
   bore – drill (n,v), dreary (n,v), carried (v)

   Note the differences in word class i.e. nouns, verbs, adjectives.

A12 IE and EI

YOU WILL NEED:
▶ Cards A12.1, enough for one set between two or three
▶ OHT A12.2
▶ Cards A12.3, enough for one set between two or three

1 Explain to the class that you are going to teach some pointers for choosing between IE and EI in spelling. Remind them that there are no hard and fast rules, but there are some good general guidelines.

2 Distribute cards A12.1 to pairs or threes, and at the same time display OHT A12.2.

3 Reassure pupils that all the words on the cards are spelt correctly and they should use them to group words together to help them to answer the questions. Allow 4-5 minutes.

4 Take feedback. Look for the following responses:

1 Which is the most common choice – IE or EI?
   IE

2 Which is commonly used at the end of words?
   IE

3 Which is commonly used at the beginning of words?
   EI

4 Which one often sounds like long A (the sound in the word DAY)?
    EI

5 Which one usually comes after C?
    EI

6 Can you spot a pattern in the exceptions to the C rule?
    Don't sound like EE

7 Which is used if GN comes after? And what meaning do these
   words share?
    EI – ruler, as in 'reign'.

5 Distribute the cards on A12.3 to pairs or threes. Read aloud a number of words from the list and ask the class to show the correct card. Allow pupils to work together and insist on a moment's thought about the answer. You can see quite quickly which pupils will need extra help or support, or if you need to go back over the rules.

A13 Vowels and double consonants

YOU WILL NEED:

▶ OHT A13.1

▶ OHT A13.2

▶ Enough white boards (these can be made from laminated A4 card) for one between two, plus marker pens and wipes

1 Show OHT A13.1 and invite pupils to say the words aloud. Remind pupils that long vowels say their own name. Point out that the words in the left column have long vowel sounds and those in the right column have short vowel sounds.

2 Ask pupils if they can see a link between the vowel sounds and the spelling of the words in both lists. Give them a minute in pairs to consider them and suggest a rule. Look for the following response: Short vowel sounds are followed by double consonants and long vowels are followed by single consonants.

3 Show OHT A13.2. Reveal the words in the left-hand column, but keep the right-hand column covered. Invite pupils in pairs to spell and show the related word on their white boards. Reveal the possible extended word on the OHT when pupils have responded. You can see at a glance if some of the pupils are still unsure.

4 Give the pupils a few minutes in pairs to consider the list of words on the right and look for patterns in the way double letters are used. Look for the response:

- short vowel + double letter + 'le' ending e.g. muddle
- base words containing a split digraph (a-e, i-e) drop the E when a vowel suffix is added, e.g. make – making, drive – driving.

A14 Softening C

YOU WILL NEED:

▶ OHT A14.1

▶ Cards A14.2, enough for one between two

1 Show OHT A14.1. Invite pupils to say the words aloud in pairs and ask what the difference is in sound between List 1 and List 2. Look for the response: The words in List 1 all have a hard C and those in List 2 have soft C sounds.

2 Give pupils 2 or 3 minutes in pairs to look for an explanation for this phenomenon. Tell them to look for patterns or letters in the words which make the C soft. You may need to give them a clue i.e. look at adjacent letters.

3 Take suggestions and look for the following response:

- C is pronounced with a soft S sound when followed by the vowels E, I and Y (which is sometimes used as a vowel). Note the soft and hard C in 'cycle', which follow the rule.

4 Distribute to pairs or threes the word cards made from A14.2 and ask pupils to search for any other patterns. Allow about 5 minutes.

5 Take suggestions and look for the following responses:

- -ence and -ance and -ice are common suffixes
- double C is usually split – a hard C at the end of the base word and a soft C at the start of the suffix e.g. accident, success.
- C wedged inside a split digraph (e.g. A-E) is soft e.g. 'face', 'twice'
- E is retained to keep the C soft if, for example, you are adding -able (noticeable).

A15 Softening G

YOU WILL NEED:

▶ OHT A15.1

▶ Cards A15.2, enough for one between two

1 Show OHT A15.1. Invite pupils to say the words aloud in pairs and ask what the difference is in sound between List 1 and List 2. Look for the response: The words in List 1 all have a hard G and those in List 2 have a soft G sound.

2 Give pupils 2 or 3 minutes in pairs to look for an explanation for this phenomenon. Tell them to look for patterns or letters in the words which make the G soft. You may need to give them a clue i.e. look at adjacent letters. You could also refer them back to the last starter, as the conventions are virtually identical.

3 Take suggestions and look for the following responses:
   • G is pronounced with a soft G sound when followed by E, I or Y.

4 Distribute to pairs or threes the word cards made from A15.2 and ask pupils to search for any other useful patterns. Allow about 5–10 minutes.

5 Take suggestions and look for the following responses:
   • soft G after D creates a short vowel sound e.g. 'judge'
   • G wedged inside a split digraph such as A-E is soft, e.g. cage/huge
   • Retain the following E to keep the G soft if, for example, you are adding a consonant suffix such as -ment (management) or -able (manageable).

A16 Hard-to-hear vowels (1)

YOU WILL NEED:

▶ OHT A16.1

▶ Handout A16.2, one between two

1 Show OHT A16.1 and explain that this session looks at hard-to-hear vowels. Ask pairs to say the words aloud to each other and see if the class can agree on their exact pronunciation.

2 Say the words aloud yourself to make them clear and ask the pupils what it is about the words which makes them hard to spell. Look for the response: Some of the vowels are hard to hear because the emphasis in the word falls elsewhere. They are not fully sounded, but skipped over lightly.

3 Remind pupils that changes in the way we pronounce words has also contributed to this quietness of vowels. The mouth tries for the easiest

way between consonants, and this means some vowels become lazy. The increasing silence of A in 'parliament' is a good example.

4 Distribute Handout A16.2 to 6 pupils in pairs to identify and underline the unstressed vowel in each word. Suggest pupils say the word aloud in pairs, first quickly and then emphasising the sound of the quiet vowel e.g. car**pet**, **de**scription.

5 Ask pupils for suggestions about the way to remember the hard-to-hear vowels. Look for the responses:
- Pronounce the word as it is spelt.
- Relate the word to others in the same family in which the letter is clearly sounded e.g. 'definite' – 'finite', 'infinity'.
- Search for base and root words e.g. 'differ' in 'different', 'geo' in 'geography'.
- Find words within words e.g. 'story' in 'history'.
- Statistics – E is the most common vowel.
- Mnemonics – e.g. I AM in PARLIAMENT.

A17 Hard-to-hear vowels (2)

YOU WILL NEED:
▶ Handout A17.1

1 Distribute Handout A17.1 and ask pupils in pairs to test each other on the spellings. The best speller in the pair should be tested first.

2 Tell pupils they can then check their own spellings and, in light pencil, put a small tick in the corner of the word boxes on the sheet to indicate those they got right. They can then concentrate on their errors.

3 Ask them to help each other to look for patterns which might help them to learn the incorrect spellings.

4 Stop them after a few minutes and ask them what kind of patterns they can see. Look, for example, for the following responses:
- Common suffixes e.g. -ence.
- Root and base words e.g. 'misery' in 'miserable'.
- Words within words e.g. 'son' in 'consonant'.

5 Remind pupils of the strategies mentioned at the end of the previous starter and ask them to learn the spellings of the words they got wrong, for homework. Use a future starter to retest, allowing pupils to tick off more words as they get them right, but leaving incorrect spellings for further testing, until they are all learnt.

A18 Revision

YOU WILL NEED:

▶ Handout A18.1

1 Distribute Handout A18.1 and allow 10 minutes to fill it in. Use an extended or separate starter to go over the answers and help pupils to identify their weak spots.

2 Answers:

1 What is the difference between short vowels and long vowels?
Long vowels say their own name
(1 mark)

2 Circle the most common ways to spell the long A:
A-E
NB: The split digraph is the most common way of forming long vowel sounds across the vowels.
(1 mark)

3 Choose between AI and AY in these words:
bargain   display   prayer   stain
(Half a mark for each correct spelling = 2 marks)

4 Write down the three most common ways of spelling the long E sound, and give an example of each.
EE – squeeze
EA – season
E-E – even
(Half a mark each = $1\frac{1}{2}$ marks)

5 Circle the correct spelling:
delete
(1 mark)

6 IE or EI? Insert the correct letters.
believe   receive   mischief   vein   foreign   ceiling
NB: EI after C
EI when it makes a long A sound
(Half a mark for each correct spelling = 3 marks)

7 Give two examples of words containing the long U which do not use the letter U at all. Two points if you use two different ways to spell long U.
EW (as in 'chew')   OO (as in 'boot')
(Half a mark each = 1 mark)

8 Insert OI/OY correctly:

poisonous   envoy   destroy   void

NB: OY at the end of a word

OI in the middle of words

(Half a mark each word = 2 marks)

9 Fill in the quiet vowels in the following words:

interest   history   definite   separate   different   business

(Half a mark each = 3 marks)

10 Why only one T in writing but two in written?

Single consonant follows a long vowel

Double consonant follows a short vowel

(1 mark)

11 Fill in double or single consonants:

Eating dinner.

Bees carry pollen.

(Half a mark each = 1 mark)

Total available marks = $17\frac{1}{2}$, plus a mark for each of the five personal spellings in Question 12. This totals 20 marks.

Section B: Plurals

B1 ES plurals

YOU WILL NEED:

▶ OHT B1.1

▶ Cards B1.2, enough for one set each or one between two

1   Remind pupils that all languages have ways of making plurals to indicate 'more than one'. In English you add S to most words but some words need other endings.

2   Show OHT B1.1 and ask pupils in pairs to explain why all the words in columns B and C have ES endings, whereas those in A use a simple S. Look for the response:

B – The base word ends in E, and S had been added as usual

C – The base word ends in a hissing or buzzing sound (X, S, CH or SH), and the plural adds an extra syllable. This makes the plural easier to say. Read the base word and plural aloud to demonstrate this point.

3   Remove the OHT and distribute the cards. Test understanding of the rule by using the following list of words. Ask pupils to show the correct S or ES. You can see at a glance if there is any confusion and you can go over particular words again.

inches

lights

punches

friends

dishes

kisses

flowers

boxes

buses

lists

sandwiches

glasses

pockets

words

patches

B2 Plurals for words ending in Y

YOU WILL NEED:

▶ OHT B2.1

▶ Handout B2.2

1 Show OHT B2.1 and point out that all the base words end in Y. Then ask them to work out why the words in the top box end in YS whereas those in the lower box change to IES. If they need a hint, suggest that they look at the letter preceding Y in the base word.

2 Take feedback and look for the following responses:
- Words ending in a vowel + Y simply add S
- Words ending in a consonant + Y change Y to I and add ES.

3 Distribute Handout B2.2 and ask pupils in pairs to apply the rules to the words on the list to make them plural. Allow 3 to 4 minutes.

4 Check answers and feedback by going through the words and getting pupils to explain how they made correct choices.

B3 Plurals for words ending in F

YOU WILL NEED:

▶ OHT B3.1

▶ Cards B3.2, enough for one set each or one between two

1 Show OHT B3.1 and ask pupils if they can work out the rule for making plurals for words ending in F and FE. Allow a couple of minutes.

2 Take feedback and look for the following responses:
- Words ending in F and FE change to VES
- Words ending in FF simply add S.

Write these on the whiteboard or OHT.

3 Distribute the cards on B3.2. Read aloud the singular forms from the list below and ask pupils in pairs to apply the rules by holding up the correct ending. You can see at a glance if there is any confusion and go over the rule again as necessary.

elf	elves
scarf	scarves
yourself	yourselves
bluff	bluffs
thief	thieves
wolf	wolves

(continued overleaf)

bailiff	bailiffs
shelf	shelves
cuff	cuffs
wife	wives
handcuff	handcuffs
cliff	cliffs

4 Write the word 'belief' on the board and point out the problem with 'believes': it can be both a verb and a noun and it is pronounced differently in each case. For example:

- He has strong beliefs.
- He believes in God.

Write up the different spellings and ask pupils if they can hear the difference in pronunciation. The same is true of 'proof' and 'proves'. Notice the change in spelling and pronunciation.

5 Point out there are a small number of nouns ending in F which simply add S, but these are usually obvious by their pronunciation:

roof – roofs

reef – reefs

chief – chiefs

brief – briefs

oaf – oafs

B4 Plurals for words ending in vowels

YOU WILL NEED:

▶ OHT B4.1

▶ Each pupil will need a blank piece of paper and colouring pens if possible

1 Explain that you are going to consider how to make a plural for words ending in a vowel. Note that this starter excludes the very large number of words which end in E because it is part of a split digraph e.g. 'love', 'hate', 'spite', but it does include other words ending in E such as 'tree'.

2 Show OHT B4.1 and admit from the outset that there is no particular reason why some end in S and some in ES. This is a case of having to learn which are which. It might be some consolation to point out how many of the words owe their spelling to the Italian language from which they came: the musical and food references are obvious.

3 Invite pupils to suggest how one might make this task easier. Look for the responses:

- By knowing the rule but learning the exceptions because they are fewer
- By finding a way to memorise them as a group of words.

4 Ask pupils to take just 4 minutes to draw on a blank sheet of paper a picture that includes the ES objects. Tell them it should be as bold and as memorable as possible, and link the objects together.

5 Share a few of the pictures and ask for the best offering to be reproduced on an A3 poster for the wall.

6 Point out that psychologists suggest that memorising is easier if you can visualise objects, especially if they are bold, colourful and attention-grabbing in any way e.g. by being strange or funny. The words can be remembered as a group if they are linked in the image.

B5 Unusual plurals

YOU WILL NEED

▶ Cards B5.1, enough for one set between two or three

1 Distribute the cards, enough sets for one between two or three, and explain that they contain words whose plurals are made without S. The task is to sort them into groups according to the way the plural is formed.
Allow 5 minutes.

2 Take feedback, drawing out the following points as you go:
- Those words which change the middle vowel are very old words, and still work as Old English did. High frequency words tend to resist modernisation.
- The IS into ES plural is Greek. It is interesting to note how many mathematical terms there are in this group.
- Pupils may well know already how many English words are derived from Latin words. It should be no surprise to find so many Latin plurals:

  A $\longrightarrow$ AE
  UM $\longrightarrow$ A
  US $\longrightarrow$ I

  Latin words are often associated with science, law and publishing.
- EAUX is a French plural, still in use.
- EN is a leftover from the language we shared with Northern Europe, and is still used in German. Notice how many of these words relate to the family, and like other high frequency words, have resisted modernisation. Note, however, that 'brethren' is dying out. There was once a parallel word for sisters but it has dropped out of use.
- Some words are identical in the plural. These are often animals.
- Some words are unique plurals e.g. 'penny' – 'pence'.

B6 Revision

YOU WILL NEED:
▶ Handout B6.1

1 Distribute Handout B6.1 and ask pupils to spend 10 minutes filling it in.

2 In an extended or separate starter, take pupils through the answers, consolidating the underlying rules.

1 When should you add an ES to make a plural?
If the base word ends in a hissing or buzzing sound.
(1 mark)

2 Add S or ES to the following words to make the plural.
benches   windows   boxes
kisses   dishes   schools
(Half a mark each = 3 marks)

3 When should you change the Y to IES to make a plural?
If it is preceded by a consonant.
(1 mark)

4 Fill in the plurals of the following words ending in Y:
journeys   holidays   countries
dictionaries   essays   babies
(Half a mark each = 3 marks)

5 Fill in the correct plurals for the following words ending in F:
wives   handcuffs
scarves   shelves
(Half a mark each = 2 marks)

6 Provide 2 plurals ending in F.
Look for words ending in double F or the exceptions listed in starter B3.
(Half a mark each = 1 mark)

7 Circle the most common plural ending for a word ending in a vowel:
(S)   ES
(1 mark)

8 Complete the plural form of the following words which end in a vowel:
radios   tomatoes
volcanoes   concertos
(Half a mark each = 2 marks)

9   Some words have unusual plurals. Write the plurals for the following:

axes   *plateaux*

cacti   *dice*

(Half a mark each = 2 marks)

10 Give plurals for:

parties

churches

wives

flies

antennae

donkeys

crises

cliffs

(Half a mark each = 4 marks)

Total available marks = 20.

Section C: Suffixes

C1 Suffixes which change the grammatical function of a word 1

YOU WILL NEED:
- ▶ OHT C1.1
- ▶ OHT C1.2

1 Use OHT C1.1 to explain that a suffix is an addition to the end of a word.

2 Ask pupils to identify the different suffixes used, and to work out how they add to or change the meaning of the word.

3 If they struggle with this, give the example of 'ful' meaning 'full of'.

4 Take suggestions, recognising good attempts to establish meaning. Look for the following responses: -hood = state or condition, -ology = science, -ise = to do, -ness = state, -fy = to make.

5 Ask the class to identify those endings that signify a verb (-ise, -ify) and adjectives (-ful) and nouns (-hood, -ness, -ology).

6 Ask the class if they can think of other examples of suffixes and establish their meaning e.g. penniless (-less = without), saintly (-ly = like). You might ask them to suggest a range of suffixes for 'hope', 'friend' and 'apology'.

7 Use OHT C1.2. Ask the pupils to turn the verbs into nouns, the nouns into verbs and the adjectives into verbs and nouns. Collect up the different suffixes on the board as they are suggested.

8 Ask pupils to record examples of suffixes:

To turn a word into a noun e.g. -hood, -er, -ness

To turn a word into a verb e.g. -ify, -ise, -ate

To turn a word into an adjective e.g. -y, -ty, -ic.

C2 Suffixes which change the grammatical function of a word 2

YOU WILL NEED:
- ▶ Cards C2.1, enough for one set between two or three pupils

1 Remind pupils about the way certain suffixes warn the reader of the word's function.

2 Distribute the sets of cards and allow pupils 3 minutes to sort the sufffixes under the headings. Encourage them to add more on the blanks.

3 Take feedback. The cards are arranged under the headings in the photocopiable master.

C3 Occupations 1

YOU WILL NEED:

▶ OHT C3.1

1 Invite pupils to generate a list of words ending in ER. Allow 2 or 3 minutes. Find out who thought of the most and get them to read aloud their list.

2 Ask the class now to group together and categorise the words by the way the ER is used. For example, one cluster of word will be those which describe a person who works at something e.g. farm – farmer, deal – dealer.

3 Draw out the following groups of words:
- Occupations e.g. 'farmer'
- Comparatives e.g. 'further', 'smaller'
- Verbs e.g. 'barter', 'answer'
- Nouns defined by their function e.g. 'floater', 'cruiser'
- Latin words e.g. 'mater, 'pater'
- Others e.g. 'water', 'crater'.

4 Focus on the 'occupations' group. Show OHT C3.1 and ask pupils if they can see patterns in the spellings. Look for the response: The ER occupations are older. The OR occupations generally belong to the service industries and senior administration. It follows that those on the left are more likely to be manual and low paid. There are significant exceptions e.g. 'sailor', 'actor'.

C4 Occupations 2

1 Use the homework from the previous starter or allow time to brainstorm a list of other suffixes which signify a trade or profession.

2 To help pupils who are stuck with this task, offer occasional words rather than suffixes, so that they have to isolate the suffix for themselves.

3 Draw out the occupation suffixes. This should throw up, among others:
- OLOGIST (study of) – psychologist, geologist
- IST (practioner) – artist, linguist, chiropodist, tourist
- MAN (official representative) – ombudsman, foreman

- WRIGHT (craftsman maker) – wheelwright, playwright
- IAN (practitioner) – physician, comedian
- IER (French profession) – costumier, carrier
- ARCH (ruler) – monarch, patriarch
- SMITH (metal worker) – locksmith, blacksmith

Write the suffixes on the board and do the rest orally.

4   Ask pupils if they can think of other professions ending in the (so far untouched) endings UR, IR and AR. This should throw up very few responses: 'burglar' and 'liar', for example.

5   In general, there are not that many words – professions or otherwise – ending in UR, IR or AR. Lead a brainstorm to identify the common ones. Examples include:

- concur, murmur, occur
- radar, pulsar, polar, exemplar, familiar, similar

Others are likely to belong to vowel trigraphs e.g. 'cent**aur**', 'ch**oir**', 'ch**air**'.

C5 SHUN endings 1

YOU WILL NEED:
▶ OHT C5.1

1   Use the top three words on OHT C5.1 to start the class off in a 2 minute brainstorm of words ending in the SHUN sound.

2   Stop them and ask them to add up how many different ways of writing SHUN they used in their lists. Look for the person with most alternatives and write them up on the board with an example, e.g.:

TION – education   SIAN – Malaysian

SION – extension   CEAN – ocean

CIAN – magician   SHION – cushion

SSION – passion   TIAN – Martian

3   If any of these do not turn up (the last three are rare) give the ending and let them think of examples. It makes a good homework.

4   Now ask pairs to look at their own lists and pose the question: If you don't know which ending to use, which one should you go for? In other words, which is the most common choice?

Look for the response: TION.

5 Use the lower half of OHT C5.1 to consider words ending in SION. Ask the class if they can see a pattern. If they get stuck, offer the clue: Look for the base word from which it is derived. It is usually a verb e.g. extend – extension. If they are still stuck, tell them to focus on the sound at the end of the base word.

6 Look for these responses:
   - SION often completes a base word which ends in the /d/ or /s/ sound.
   - Many people can hear the difference of the soft shush in passion and the Z sound in fusion. These are distinct sounds which can act as clues when pupils are uncertain.

7 Move on to the next starter to complete this work.

C6 SHUN endings 2

YOU WILL NEED:

▶ The list of words pupils generated in the last starter
▶ OHT C6.1
▶ A dictionary per pair

1 Ask pupils if they can think of any other words ending in SIAN besides Malaysian. After a few moments, give the clue: think of nationalities. This may throw up: Russian, Persian, Indonesian, Prussian, Asian, Polynesian, Parisian, Caucasian – these are all nationalities and are a good way to remember the use of SIAN.

   NB: Grecian is an exception.

2 If you have covered IC endings recently, invite pupils to remember which words end in CIAN. If not, prompt them with the idea of jobs. This will lead to the words on OHT C6.1.

   If it is new to them, offer OHT C6.1 and ask them if they can see any patterns in the words ending in CIAN. Look for the responses:
   - The base word ends in IC or ICS
   - CIAN reltes to jobs.

3 Finally write up the three untouched endings: TIAN, CEAN, SHION and allow 2 to 3 minutes for groups of four to compete against others to list words using these endings. They must check in the dictionary before listing. They may produce:

crustacean

ocean

Martian

Venetian

fashion

cushion

C7 Consonant suffixes

YOU WILL NEED:

▶ OHT C7.1

1 Reveal the top section of the OHT and point out that this is a list of suffixes with something in common: they all start with a consonant. You could ask pupils to give you no more than two or three examples of words which use these suffixes.

2 Put pupils into groups of four and reveal the rest of the OHT. Issue a challenge to write down as many words as they can by matching the suffixes at the top of the page with the words at the bottom. Allow 4 or 5 minutes.

3 Stop and draw pupils' attention to the listing of words on the OHT. They are in four groups:
   • Words ending in a consonant
   • Words ending in E
   • Words ending in consonant + Y
   • Words ending in vowel + y

4 Ask them to come up with the rule about adding consonant suffixes and the only major exception to it. Allow 1 minute.

5 Take feedback. Look for the response: Just add the suffix unless it ends in consonant + Y, in which case change the Y to I before adding.

6 Ask pupils what strategy they might use to remember this exception. The answer lies in identifying a key word they do know and using this as a point of reference.

C8 Vowel suffixes

YOU WILL NEED

▶ OHT C8.1

1 Remind pupils of the suffixes studied last lesson, and explain that this is a repeat activity but this time with suffixes that start with vowels.

2 The task is to work out the rules for each set of words. Allow 3 or 4 minutes.

3 Take feedback and look for the responses:
   • Most words just add the suffix
   • Words ending in E: drop the E. This is to avoid having two vowels. The words need a vowel, but the new one will do.
   • Words ending in consonant + Y change the Y to I as they do for consonant suffixes.

C9 Compounding full, all and till

1 Write the three words on the board:

full

all

till

2 Explain that the purpose of this starter is to learn what happens to these words when they are compounded with others.

3 Challenge pupils in groups of four to come up with as many words as they can think of in 1 minute which build 'all' and 'till' into longer words e.g. 'pitiful', 'always'.

4 Take feedback. Look for:
- until
- always, also, altogether, although, almost

5 Ask what has happened to the words 'till' and 'all' in these spellings: they have lost an L.

6 Now ask if the same is true of the very many words ending in 'full'. It is.

7 Use the word 'fulfil' to illustrate how the same thing happens if 'full' appears at the beginning.

8 For an able group, you can move on to distinguish between these words and separate words such as:

hand full (hand is full)

handful (a measure)

all right (all correct)

alright (okay)

Context provides the clue, and a way of checking is to see if one of the words would stand alone, e.g. 'The answers are (all) right'.

C10 Modifying words ending in Y

YOU WILL NEED:
- ▶ OHT C10.1
- ▶ OHT C10.2

1 Show OHT C10.1. Point out that the words in List 1 end in Y but do not change when a suffix is added.

2 Point out that the words in List 2 also end in Y but *do* change when a suffix is added.

3 Pose the question: What has happened to the Y in List 2? Look for the response that the Y has changed to an I.

4 Follow up immediately with: Why has the Y changed to an I? Allow pairs 1 minute to come up with an hypothesis. Look for the response that Y changes to I if the base word ends in consonant + Y.

Remind pupils that adding -ing to a word ending in Y is an exception to the rule e.g. 'supplying'. If the class are on the ball, ask them to explain why. The answer might involve using the visually disturbing double I in the word 'suppliing'.

5 Show OHT C10.2 and ask pupils to identify the four words in the list which would not change if a suffix were added. Look for the answers: play, boy, enjoy and way, because the Y is preceded by a vowel.

C11 Changing letters

YOU WILL NEED:
▶ OHT C11.1

1 Display the OHT and explain to pupils that all these words have a habit of changing key letters when they add certain suffixes. Go through the list of words, asking for suggestions about the following spellings and why they might change letters:

- evocation, provocation
- wolves, knives, loaves (to reflect the easier pronunciation)
- decision, extension, erosion (verbs ending in D or DE change to SION)
- panicking, frolicking, picnicking (to keep the hard /c/ sound)
- receipt (an affectation borrowed from the Latin)
- curiosity, generosity (to avoid an awkward vowel sound – note also glamour, vigour, humour and rigour which do the same thing)

2 Allow the class a minute or so in groups to think of further words in which letters change. They may suggest large groups of words such as words which drop vowels when suffixes are added e.g.

announce – annunciation
pronounce – pronunciation
example – exemplify
disaster – disastrous
hunger – hungry
anger – angry
enter – entrance
exclaim – exclamation
proclaim – proclamation

compel – compulsion

expel – expulsion

propel – propulsion

C12 Able or ible 1

YOU WILL NEED:

▶ OHT C12.1

▶ Cards C12.2 prepared as pairs of flashcards, enough for one set each

1 Show OHT C12.1 and point out the way the words on the left end in -able and the others end in -ible.

2 Pose the question: Why do these words end in -able and these in -ible? Allow the class 1 minute in pairs or threes to come up with a hypothesis.

3 If they struggle with this, give them the clue: Look at the base word e.g. 'rely' in 'reliable'.

4 Take suggestions, rewarding good observation and attempts to find patterns. Look for the following responses:

- If there is a recognisable base word, use -able.
- If you can rephrase it to 'Be able to…' (e.g. able to bend, able to rely), use -able.
- If you can hear the difference, saying the word will help you.
- If in doubt, choose -able: it is much more common.

5 Issue to each pupil a pair of flashcards made from Handout C12.2: one for -able and one for -ible, and ask pupils to show the correct ending for each of these words as you read them aloud:

- adaptable
- disposable
- invisible
- enviable
- payable
- impossible
- irascrible (they can work this out)
- variable
- possible

If there is another adult in the classroom, ask them to sit at the front and note down those pupils who make errors, so you know where to target further work.

C13 Able or ible 2

YOU WILL NEED:

▶ OHT C13.1

1   Recapitulate the guidance in the last starter about deciding on -able or -ible.

2   Show OHT C13.1 and ask pupils to spot the four exceptions to the rule. They should find: 'sensible', 'responsible', 'accessible' and 'probable'.

3   Ask if they can see any patterns in the exceptions.
   • Most base word ending in S use -ible ('sensible', 'responsible', 'accessible')
   • The high frequency exceptions must be learnt ('probable').

4   Ask why the word reliable features an I rather than a Y. (Like all words ending in Y, the Y has changed to I when a suffix is added.)

5   Ask why there is still an E in the middle of 'manageable' (keeps the G soft), and 'noticeable' (keeps the C soft).

C14 Cede, ceed, sede and seed endings

YOU WILL NEED:

▶ Cards C14.1, enough for one set between two or three

1   Distribute the word cards made from C14.1 and explain to pupils that they contain word parts for words ending in the 'seed' sound. Allow 5 minutes for pupils to match up the word parts, and group the words using the same ending.

2   Distribute the four definitions cards made from C14.1 and ask pupils to allocate them to the correct word group.

3   To debrief, take 'seed' first. Pupils may be familiar with 'linseed oil', 'aniseed sweets' and 'birdseed'.

4   Next identify the odd one out: 'supersede' and ask if anyone knows its meaning: 'to replace'.

5   This leaves the more tricky 'ceed' and 'cede' options. Take 'ceed' first and tell pupils that although there are very few words that take this ending, they are high frequency words. Ask if anyone is sure they know a word taking this ending. Your better spellers might be confident to say 'succeed', 'proceed' and 'exceed'. You can point out the mnemonic word SPEED (S for succeed, P for proceed, E for exceed and EED for the ending: it works for some people). This ending means 'go beyond'.

6 This leaves 'cede' endings. These words are rarely used in everyday conversation, but there are more of them. Work out this ending by process of elimination.

C15 IC endings

YOU WILL NEED:

▶ OHT C15.1

1 Brainstorm words ending in IC, e.g. 'ironic', 'caustic', 'fantastic', 'basic' and 'mystic'.

2 Establish that the IC stem is often used to make a word an adjective. Demonstrate how the meaning can be worked out from the base word e.g. base + ic.

3 Use OHT C15.1 keeping the right-hand column covered. Ask the pupils to provide the word and spelling for a person who practices these skills. Reveal answers as you go.

4 Establish that words ending in IC add IAN to create the -ician ending.

5 Ask why the C goes soft in -ician. Look for the response: Because it is followed by a vowel.

C16 L endings 1

YOU WILL NEED:

▶ Cards C16.1, enough for one set between two or three
▶ OHT C16.2

1 Explain that you are going to explore words ending in the /l/ sound. The focus will be on the choice between LE, EL and AL in the final syllable. Acknowledge at the outset that there are no absolute rules, but certainly there are groups of words which tend to take one rather than the other ending.

2 Distribute the cards and ask pupils to spread them out. Then ask them to organise the cards into groups with a similar pattern to see if they can come up with any rules.

3 After a few minutes, put up OHT C16.2 which contains questions to help them group the cards and draw conclusions.

4 Allow 2 more minutes and take feedback on the questions:
- Which ending is the most common? – LE
- Which ending is most often used after double letters? – LE
- Which endings are part of common suffixes? -ABLE, -IBLE
- Which ending follows a recognisable base word? – AL (often added as a second suffix to -TION and -IC endings)
- Which ending is used for words that clearly rhyme with HELL? – EL

C17 L endings 2

1 Explain that in the last starter you explored LE, EL and AL endings. In this starter, you will look at other ways of making the L ending. Draw out from pupils what these are by combining L with the remaining vowels: IL, OL, UL. As before, the /l/ sound is the final syllable (thus excluding OOL for example).

2 Set a challenge to pupils in groups to think of as many suitable words as they can in 2 minutes.

3 Take feedback, rewarding interesting and correctly spelt words. Look for:

IL: tendril, evil, devil, anvil, pencil, fossil

OL: alcohol, idol, carol, petrol, parasol

UL: annul, all words ending in FUL

D1 Adding prefixes

YOU WILL NEED:

▶ OHT D1.1

1 Show OHT D1.1 and explain that the prefixes on the left can be added to the words on the right to alter their meanings. Ask pupils to work out the meaning of the three prefixes featured in the OHT. Look for:

- dis = not
- pre= before
- re = again

2 As an example, do the first 'word sum' (dis + appear =) on the board but pause after 'dis' and ask the class which letter comes next. Explain that some people wonder whether there should be a single or a double S. Look for the correct answer (a single S in disappear) and explain that prefixes are very simple because they do not affect spellings in the way suffixes do. They are simply added to whatever is there.

3 Repeat this approach for the second word sum, 'dissatisfied', so that pupils can understand that the first S is part of the prefix, whereas the second S is part of the root – hence two Ss.

4 Continue with the other word sums.

5 Stop at 'pre-empt' and 're-educate' and note that the prefix ends in a vowel, and the base word starts with a vowel. To avoid creating an 'ee' digraph, the two vowels are divided by a hyphen.

6 Stop at 'preface' to note the change in pronunciation when the root and prefix are compounded.

7 Stop at 'revise' to point out that although 'vise' is not a free-standing word, a knowledge of root meanings (vise = look) can suggest the meaning (revise = to look at again). This is a useful technique to use on unfamiliar vocabulary.

8 Now conduct a spot spelling test:
- How many Ns in unnecessary?
- How many Ns in unacceptable?
- How do you spell prehistoric?
- How do you spell re-enter?
- How do you spell disagree?
- How do you spell disservice?

D2 Prefix game

YOU WILL NEED:

▶ Cards D2.1, enough for one card each

1 Distribute the cards made from D1.2, one to each pupil. Keep one card for yourself as the 'starter'. Begin by reading aloud the prefix printed on the bottom half of your card.

2 One pupil should have the matching base word on the top half of their card, which they read aloud to answer.

3 The same pupil continues, by reading aloud the prefix printed on the bottom half of their card. Another pupil will answer by reading the appropriate base word from the top half of their card and so on until the chain is unable to go any further. The aim is to use all the cards in one turn, ending with the person who started.

4 A good extension is to put pupils in groups to generate further loops for the class to try.

D3 Number prefixes

YOU WILL NEED:

▶ OHT D3.1

▶ Handout D3.2

1 Show OHT D3.1 but keep it covered for a moment whilst you remind pupils that some prefixes denote numbers. Reveal; each word at a time and draw out the following points as you go:

bicycle – Which part of the word tells us that the vehicle has two wheels?
● bi = Greek for two.

tricycle – How many wheels?
● Three. Tri = Greek for three.

octopus – why 'octo'?
● octo = Latin for eight.

Octavius Caesar – How did his parents choose his name?
● He was their eighth child.

triceratops – Why was the dinosaur given this name?
● It has three horns. Tri = three Cera = horn.

millenium – How many years in a millennium?
Mille = 1000

2 Distribute Handout D3.2 and ask pupils to complete it in groups, or for homework.

Prefix	Number	Examples
uni	1	unicorn unicycle universe
mono	1	monotonous monopoly monogamy
bi	2	bicarbonate bicycle binary
duo	2	duet duel duo
tri	3	tricycle triangle tripod
quad	4	quadrant quadrilateral quadrangle
pent	5	pentagon pentameter pentathlete
sept	7	September septuplets septuagenarian
oct	8	octopus octagon October
dec	10	decimal December decimate
cent	100	century centimetre centurion
mill	1000	millennium million millilitre

D4 Latin prefixes

YOU WILL NEED:

▶ OHT D4.1

▶ Handout D4.2, enough for one between two

1 Show OHT D4.1 and ask pupils to work out what the prefixes means by finding the common thread of meaning.

2 Take feedback, rewarding sensible suggestions. Look for the following responses:

- Act = do
- Sense = feel
- Terr = earth.

3 Now allow 2 minutes while pupils brainstorm other words beginning with these prefixes. Take feedback and confirm that the words contain the meaning in the prefix.

4 Distribute copies of Handout D4.2 and ask pupils to work in pairs to complete the boxes.

- aqua (water) aquarium, aquatic, aquamarine, aqueduct
- audi (hear) audible, auditory, audience, audition
- cap (head) captain, capital, decapitate
- dent (tooth) dentist, dental, indent
- grat (please) gratitude, gratify, grateful
- liber (free) liberate, liberal, liberty
- lum (light) luminous, luminary, illuminate
- man (hand) manufacture, manipulate, manual, manuscript
- mari (sea) maritime, marine, submarine, mariner
- mem (mindful) memory, remember, memento
- min (small) minimum, minute, minus, minor
- mot (move) motor, motion, motive, motivate
- multi (many) multiply, multitude, multiple, multiplicity
- nov (new) novice, novel, novelty, innovate
- ped (foot) pedal, pedestrian, pedestal
- sign (mark) sign, signature, signal, insignia, significant
- sta (stand) stationary, stagnant, statue, stable, stand
- tempo (time) temporary, temporal, tempo
- vac (empty) vacate, vacuum, vacuous, vacant.

5 You may like to turn the activity into a game and award points for each correct word, two points for each correct meaning, and one point for a good guess at the meaning.

D5 Common antonyms

1 Write the word 'happy' on the board and ask the class to provide the prefix that makes it mean the opposite, i.e. un + happy.

2 Explain that an **antonym** is an opposite, and that most antonyms are made by adding a prefix like UN.

3 Allow the class 1 minute in groups to brainstorm as many words as they can which make their antonyms using UN, (e.g. undone, unnecessary, undignified, unfair, unpopular). Praise groups who think of several examples.

4 Now ask the class to take a minute in the same groups to come up with other antonym prefixes, e.g. anti (see list below for possible answers).

5 Now allocate an antonym prefix for each group and allow them 2 minutes to come up with a list of words using the prefix.
Possible answers:
- anti (antibiotic, antidote).
- de (demist, decode)
- mis (mistreat, misbehave)
- dis (disprove, dissatisfied)
- non (non-stick, non-existent)
- ir (irresponsible, irreversible)
- in (incapable, insecure)
- a (amoral, abnormal)
- im (impossible, impassable)
- il (illegal, illogical).

6 In taking feedback, ask groups what they notice about the words in the list. Draw out spelling patterns:
- il + words starting with L
- ir + words starting with R
- im + words starting with M and P
- hyphens often follow 'anti' and 'non'.

Also note that antonym prefixes have particular nuances, e.g.
- 'un' means 'not'
- 'de' means 'undo'
- 'mis' means 'wrong' or 'false'
- 'non' means 'not'
- 'anti' means 'against'.

E1 Root words

YOU WILL NEED:
- OHT E1.1
- OHT E1.2
- Plain white sheet of paper between two pupils; A3 works best

1 Show OHT E1.1 and explain that a root is a word part with a particular meaning because it is drawn from a classical word, e.g. Latin or Greek. As you explain this to the pupils, point to the roots in the words on OHT E1.1: 'form', 'spec', 'port' and 'circ'.

2 Ask pupils to suggest meanings of each root. Reward good attempts, and fill in the answers.
   - 'form' means 'shape'
   - 'spec' means 'to see'
   - 'port' means 'carry'
   - 'circ' means 'round'.

3 Show OHT E1.2 which shows the start of a word web. Discuss the way the web has been constructed, i.e. from the roots 'bio' (life) and 'ology' (science or study). To construct a web, pupils must find exactly two words which have the same root with the same meaning, and must be able to say what the root means. Some pupils may be able to see how the web could be extended from the root 'anto' in antibiotic (e.g. by adding anticlockwise, antidote) or 'astro' in astrology (e.g. by adding astronomy, asteroid).

4 Work for a minute or so extending the web on the OHT wherever pupils can see an opportunity. The purpose is to demonstrate how to extend the web.

5 Now ask pupils to get into twos or threes and write the word 'construct' in the middle of a large clean piece of paper. Draw out the meanings (con = together, struct = build). Allow 4 or 5 minutes for pupils to create a word web based on this word.

E2 More word webs

YOU WILL NEED:
- Clean sheets of plain paper, enough for one each

1 Put pupils into groups of four, each pupil with a blank sheet of paper.

2 Remind pupils about the word web created last lesson, and give each group four words, one for each sheet:

- bicycle (bi = two, cycle = rotate, round)
- telephone (tele = distant, phon = sound)
- microscope (micro = tiny, scope = see)
- benefactor (bene = good, fac(t) = make or do).

Each pupil takes charge of a word, but draws on the other three for ideas. Allow approximately 8 minutes.

3 Display good examples.

E3 Common roots

YOU WILL NEED:
▶ OHT E3.1
▶ Handout E3.2

1 Show OHT E3.1 and ask pupils to fill in the table using suggestions from the class. Provide three words containing the root and the meaning.
- mobil (to move) mobile, automobile, mobility, immobile
- sect (cut) dissect, bisect, section, sector
- spir (breathe) respiration, inspire, conspire, spirit.

2 Distribute copies of Handout E3.2. Working in pairs, pupils are to construct a similar chart, providing the meaning and three examples. Allow a few minutes.

3 Take feedback.

- dict (means speak) dictionary, dictate, predict, contradict
- ten (means hold) tenure, tenacious, tenant, retentive
- tex (means weave) texture, context, text, textile
- tract (means pull) tractor, subtract, attract, retract
- vit (means live) survive, vital, vitamin, revive
- void (means empty) void, devoid, avoid, avoidance
- volv (means to roll) revolve, revolution, involve, evolve.

E4 The spelling of roots

YOU WILL NEED:
▶ OHT E4.1
▶ Handout E4.2

1 Show OHT E4.1 and ask pupils in pairs to work out the meaning of the root in each group. After a minute or so, take suggestions. Look for:
- flex/flect: bend

- jud/just: judge
- vid/vis: see.

3 Draw attention to the way the spelling of the root varies, e.g. jud/just, and ask pupils why this might be. Look for the response:

- Like many spellings, these have changed over time.
- Like many spellings, the ending of a root can change depending on the suffix.

4 Distribute copies of Handout E4.2 , in which pupils are provided with the root and its meaning. Alert pupils to the fact that all these roots change slightly in their spellings from word to word. Pupils can be sure they have the correct root if they check that each word carries the meaning stated. Allow a few minutes for pairs to complete the word boxes.

5 Identify the pair with the highest number of words and take their answers, checking that the word carries the root meaning and pointing out variations in spelling.

ROOT	MEANING	WORD 1	WORD 2	WORD 3	WORD 4
mit/mis	send	mission	transmit	missile	emit
pel/pul	drive	propel	expel	compulsion	impulse
pens/pend	hang	pendant	depend	pedulum	suspend
cur/cour	run	courier	excursion	current	recur
voc/voic/vok	call	voice	invoke	vocal	provoke
ped/pod	foot	pedal	podium	pedestrian	quadruped
scrib/scrip	write	scripture	scribble	scribe	inscription

Section F: Apostrophes

F1 The omission apostrophe

YOU WILL NEED:
▶ OHT F1.1

1 Show OHT F1.1 and pose the question: What is the difference between the words in the left-hand column and those in the right-hand column?

2 Take suggestions, and look for the following responses:

- The words in the right-hand column have letters omitted.
- The words in the right-hand column are contractions of the words in the left-hand column.
- The words in the right-hand column have gained apostrophes.
- The apostrophes show where there are letters missing.

3 Explain explicitly that contractions are formed where two or more words are joined and some letters missed out. The apostrophe stands in the place of the missing letter or letters.

4 Pose the question: Can you see any contractions that don't follow the same patterns as the others? Take suggestions, rewarding good observations and look for the response: 'Won't' and 'Shan't' are unusual because the full forms have been modified.

5 Pose the question: Why would a writer want to use contractions in their work? Look carefully at the last three examples. Why do you think contractions have been used here? Take suggestions, rewarding good observations and look for the following responses:

- Contractions occur most frequently in spoken and informal language so the writer might use contractions to recreate an authentic sound of a spoken voice.
- In the last three examples, the contractions create a 'catchy' rhythm as they don't have to be articulated as much as the original 'full forms' – handy for advertisers and poets.

F2 The possessive apostrophe

YOU WILL NEED:
▶ OHT F2.1

1 Show the top line of OHT F2.1 but keep the rest covered.

2 Explain that the apostrophe followed by the letter S shows belonging. For example, 'My brother's car'. This is very straightforward.

3 Show the middle section OHT F2.1 and ask pupils to suggest where to place the apostrophe in each case.

4 Show the lower section of OHT F2.1 and ask pupils to reformulate the phrases using a possessive apostrophe:

The rabbit belongs to Sam. (Sam's rabbit)

The book belongs to Tim. (Tim's book)

The car belongs to Mr. Anscombe. (Mr Anscombe's car)

The scooter belongs to the boy. (The boy's scooter)

The house belongs to my uncle. (My uncle's house)

5 Finally, ask pupils working in pairs to write at least five advertising phrases which use apostrophes to show simple possession for some of their favourite commodities. Examples might include chocolate bars, sports equipment, ice cream, details about a local radio station, fashion items, etc.

If pupils find this difficult, provide them with these examples:

- Sam's Ice Cream Parlour.
- Jane's Sports Shop.
- Cadbury's great taste.
- Radio London's local news.

Reward pairs who have included more than five and discuss interesting examples.

F3 Its and it's

YOU WILL NEED:

▶ OHT F3.1

▶ Cards F3.2, enough for one set between two

1 Write 'its' and 'it's' onto the board and explain that this is an important construction to get right because we use it all the time. Remind pupils that 'it's' means 'it is' or 'it has'.

2 Show OHT F3.1 and ask pupils to work out whether the word 'it's' means 'it is' or 'it has'. Point out the value of mental substitution as a way of checking instinctive answers.

- It has been a cold night.
- It is colder than yesterday.
- It has been a year since I saw him.
- It is going to be a close finish.
- It is a good job we came prepared.
- Look carefully at the insect and you'll see it is still alive.
- We found treasure where it has been buried for hundreds of years.
- The dog ran away. It has been missing for days.

- It is a wonder that anyone survived the storm.
- We sheltered where it is safe.

3 Distribute the two cards on F3.2 to each pair in the class and ask them to hold up the correct version in response to the following sentences which you read out:

- It's too far to go.
- The rabbit stayed in its hutch.
- It's too close for comfort.
- Did you see the bear in its cage?
- It's Tuesday and it's Quiz Night!
- My dog eats its own tail!
- It's too late, baby.
- It's my turn.

F5 Possessive plurals

YOU WILL NEED:
▶ OHT F4.1

1 Show the top section of OHT F4.1 and pose the question: Why is the apostrophe added after the S in these cases? Look for the answer that if the ownership is plural, the apostrophe goes after the S at the end of the word.

2 Now show the middle section of the OHT and ask why the apostrophe in this case goes before the S even though it is a plural? Look for the response: If the word is plural and the word does not end in S, add the apostrophe and an S. Draw out some other words where this might apply e.g. 'the children's parties'; 'the men's changing rooms'; 'the women's shoes'.

3 Show the lower section of the OHT and ask them to distinguish between the meanings of the paired phrases.

4 Pose these phrases orally and ask pupils to spell aloud the apostrophised word, to show how the apostrophe is applied:

- The King's head
- The dog's dinner (one dog)
- The children's books
- The man's jacket
- The man's jackets
- The lady's slipper (one lady)
- The ladies' room (several ladies).

Section G: Homophones

G1 Homophones

YOU WILL NEED:

▶ OHT G1.1

▶ Handout G1.2

1 Show the top section of OHT G1.1. Discuss the joke. It relies on the fact that 'pair' and 'pear' sound the same, though they are spelt differently. These words are called **homophones**.

2 Show the lower section of OHT G1.1 and ask pupils to distinguish between the words in each set.

3 Offer the definition: A homophone is a word which sounds the same as another, but is spelt differently.

4 Pose the question: How can you remember which spelling is which? Allow 2 minutes for discussion in pairs and take suggestions. For example:

- Bear: Bears Enjoy A Rest. Air, heir: Air Is Right/ Heir Enjoys Interesting Riches.
- Use word families: Where, there, here (have the 'here' string in common).

5 Distribute copies of Handout G1.2. In pairs, pupils must come up with mnemonics for as many of the pairs as they can. Allow 5 minutes then take feedback. Some of the responses might merit wall posters.

G2 Two, too and to

YOU WILL NEED:

▶ OHT G2.1

▶ Cards G2.2, enough for one set each or one between two

1 Show OHT G2.1 and ask pupils for the correct spellings to insert into the gaps.

It was *too* early.

He wanted *to* go home.

She bought *two* tomato pizzas.

2 Ask pupils to come up with a way of remembering which is which. For example:

- TWO goes with TWICE.
- TOO means excessive – it even has a double O.
- TO goes with DO because it is often part of a verb – when you want *to do* something.

- TO goes with GO because it also means towards, e.g. *Go to* work.
- TO is the most common.

4   Distribute the cards made from G2.2 to each pupil, then read aloud the sentences below and ask them to show the correct card.

- Forty thousand spectators turned up to watch.
- To be or not to be.
- The game was lost within two minutes.
- The cake was too tempting.
- Let's go to the match.
- Do you have any cards to swap?
- He played football too much.
- You have two choices.
- She was chosen to play in the first team.
- Let me come, too.
- A holiday to remember.
- No-one knows the way to go.
- There are two ways out of the maze.
- Got to stop now!

G3 Common homophones

YOU WILL NEED:

▶ Handout G3.1, enough for one each
▶ Handout G3.2, enough for one each

1   Distribute Handout G3.1 to each pupil and ask everyone to tick the homophone pairs or groups that they are confident of using accurately in their writing, but leave unticked those that they know – or suspect – cause them confusion.

2   Now ask them to transfer the confusing homophones into the left-hand column of Handout G3.2, and use the right-hand column to devise a mnemonic or way of distinguishing the spellings.

3   Share three or four examples with the whole class, highlighting the merits of the chosen strategy or suggesting improvements.

4   In a future starter, ask pupils to test each other on the unticked homophones. If the answer is correct, it can be ticked off. If not, leave it unticked for further testing.

Section H: Unusual word families

H1 Ough and ought

YOU WILL NEED:

▶ Cards H1.1, enough for one between two or three

1 Distribute a set of word cards made from H1.1 and ask the pupils to sort them into piles depending on the pronunciation of the 'ough' letter string. Note that local accents should be accepted and taken into account. Look for the following responses:
   - tough, rough, enough
   - through
   - trough, cough
   - plough, drought
   - thought, sought, ought
   - though, although
   - thorough.

2 Ask the pupils if they can add any more words to each category. For example: bough, bought, nought.

3 Ask pupils to brainstorm words containing 'augh' and do a similar exercise on the board together or on paper in groups.
   - laugh, laughter, draught
   - caught, fraught, haughty, naughty.

H2 Eigh and eight

1 Remind pupils of the investigations into 'ough' and 'augh' words in the last starter and ask them to brainstorm words containing the letter string 'eigh'. Tell them that they are looking for eight or more in common use.
   Allow 2 minutes.

2 Draw out the list:
   Weigh, sleigh, neigh, eight, weight, freight, height, neigh, neighbour.

3 Now ask pupils to group them by sound, remembering to accept local pronunciation.

4 Next ask pupils to devise ways of remembering words in this list that they know they get wrong. This might include rhymes, puzzles, mnemonics, etc. (e.g. He eats in giant houses tall.) Hear some of these suggestions and reward inventive methods.

H3 Quiet consonants

YOU WILL NEED:
- ▶ OHT H3.1
- ▶ OHT H3.2

1. Explain that you are going to consider ways of remembering quiet consonants. Reveal one by one the words on the top section of OHT H3.1, asking pupils at first to identify the quiet consonant, and why it is there. You could ask pupils to spell the word in advance of showing it. Discuss as you go the way one can remember the correct spelling.
   - *Wednesday* – named after the Norse God – Woden's Day. Many people remember by pronouncing the syllables as they are spelt.
   - *Raspberry* – rasp is the type of berry.
   - *Muscle* – the silent C can be identified through the related word muscular, in which the C is pronounced.
   - *Design* – the silent G can be identified through the related word designated, in which the G is pronounced.
   - *Cupboard* – another compound word – a board was the word used for a wooden shelf.
   - *Christmas* – the T is more apparent in the base word Christ.
   - *Handbag* – an example of a compound word in which the D is disappearing.

2. Draw out explicitly the three ways of recalling the quiet consonants:
   1. Pronounce the word as it is spelt.
   2. Relate the word to others in the same family in which the letter is clearly sounded.
   3. Search for compounded base words.

3. Point out that quiet consonants are the result of ongoing change in the way people speak the language. Spellings were fixed by the dictionary several hundred years ago, but the way we pronounce words has continued to change. It is remarkable to realise that at one time, most words were pronounced as they are spelt.

4. Point out that many silent consonants are simply part of a digraph. A digraph is a single sound represented by two letters, thus creating a seemingly silent letter. Three examples they will know instantly are TH, SH and CH, but these are rarely confused because they create an entirely new sound unrelated to the two letters. The problem comes when the sound made by the digraph is associated with one of the letters e.g. WRITE – the WR makes a sound like R.

5. Reveal the lower section of OHT H3.1 and ask pupils to suggest two or three additional examples in each case.

6 Show OHT H3.1 and ask pupils to identify and if possible explain the quiet consonant in each word.

H4 Unusual consonant digraphs 1

YOU WILL NEED:

▶ OHT H4.1

▶ Handout H4.2 on card

▶ Handout H4.3

1 Show OHT H4.1 and explain that these are all examples of digraphs. Explain that the word digraph refers to a group of two letters representing one sound.

2 Explain that some digraphs sound nothing like either of the letters in them e.g. TH – it is a new sound. Others like KN borrow the sound from just one letter. Ask them to pick out which are which.

3 Distribute Handouts H4.2 and H4.3 to groups of two or three, and ask pupils to construct their spinners using a pencil as a spinner.

4 Pupils now take turns in their group to use the spinner. The player must insert into Handout H3.3 a new word containing the resulting digraph. They also keep an individual tally of points scored.

- 1 Point for: 'gn', 'kn', 'mb'

- 2 Points for: 'pt', 'ps', 'pn'

NB: The use of dictionaries is discretionary.

Words where the letters are not used as a digraph are not allowed e.g. amber, laptop.

kn	ps	gn	pt	mb	pn
know	psychic	gnaw	pterodactyl	lamb	pneumatic
knowledge	psychiatrist	gnashed	ptarmigan	limb	pneumonia
knit	psychiatry	gnat	ptosis	tomb	pneumonic
knuckle	psychiatric	gnarled	ptyalin	aplomb	
knight	psycho	gnome	Receipt	dumb	
knickers	psychology	resign		bomb	
knock	psyche	foreign		comb	
knife	psalm	reign		plumb	
knead	pseudonym	design		thumb	
knell		sign		numb	
knot		align		crumb	
knee		arraign		womb	
knob		sovereign			
knack					

Note that 'receipt' features an unusual diagraph at the end of the word.

H5 Unusual consonant digraphs 2

YOU WILL NEED:

▶ Handout H5.1

1 Remind pupils about the unusual digraphs in the last starter and allow 2 minutes to brainstorm any more unusual or uncommon examples. Circulate around the groups providing clues to get them going if they get stuck. Look for:

- WR – wrist, write, wrinkle
- LM – calm, embalm, qualms, salmon, psalm,
- BT – subtle, doubt
- MN – mnemonic
- SW – answer, sword
- GH – ghost, ghastly
- ST – whistle, castle, thistle, wrestle.

Remember to distinguish between digraphs (one sound) and when the letters are used for individual sounds (blends).

2 Distribute Handout H4.1 and invite pupils to fill in the crossword which contains WR words. They could construct their own crossword using a different digraph. The complete crossword should look like this:

Section I: Learning strategies

I1 Creating acronyms

1 Explain the term **acronym**: each letter in a word stands for another word, e.g. NASA, UNESCO. The idea can be used to recall spellings. For example:

- BECAUSE: Billy Eats Cake And Usually Sucks Eggs.
- NECESSARY: Not Every Child Enjoys Sticky Sweets And Remains Young.

2 Ask pupils if they know any others.

3 Ask pupils to create acronyms for:

- IMMEDIATE
- RHYTHM

Share suggestions. The best acronyms are apt and funny.

4 Ask pupils to think of two words they find difficult to spell. Check the spellings and then ask them to invent their own acronyms for the words.

I2 Referring to related words

YOU WILL NEED:

▶ OHT I2.1

1 Explain that you are going to learn a way to remember tricky letters in words by referring to related words.

2 Show the top section of OHT I2.1 and use 'sign' as an example. Although the G is silent, it is pronounced in the related words: 'signature' and 'signal'. The three can be packaged together in a sentence for easier recall.

3 Show the rest of the OHT and ask pupils to take a few minutes to find related words which would help to remember the problematic underlined letters.

Muscle – muscular

Medicine – medical

Definite – finite, infinity

There – here, where

Heard – ear, hear

Bomb – bombastic, bombadier.

13 Words within words

YOU WILL NEED:
▶ OHT I3.1

1 Explain that another useful way to remember the tricky parts of words is to find another, simpler word within them.

2 Demonstrate using the top section of OHT I3.1 to find 'ear' in 'h<u>ear</u>d' and 'here' in '<u>there</u>'.

3 Show 'vegetable' in the middle section of the OHT and allow groups 1 minute to find as many words within it as they can (get, table, tab, able).

   Point out the usefulness of the word GET because it pinpoints the correct vowel.

4 Reveal the rest of the words on the OHT and ask pupils to find useful words within them that would help to pinpoint the tricky letters.
   - Knowledge – know and ledge
   - Separate – there's 'a rat' in separate
   - Business – business is a sin
   - Library – bra (!)
   - Island – there is land
   - Environment – iron
   - Parliament – I am Liam
   - Definite – finite, nit
   - Immediate – media, ate
   - Piece – piece of pie
   - Temperature – temper, rat.

14 Mnemonics

YOU WILL NEED:
▶ OHT I4.1

1 Explain that even the most unusual words can sometimes be learnt if you can find something memorable in them.

2 Use OHT I4.1 to stimulate some examples and ideas. Do the first two and let the class suggest the rest:

   February - RU in FebRUary?

   Necessary – one **c**ollar, two **s**leeves

   Friend – I'll be your friend to the end

   Stationary - A **car** is station**ary**

   Stationery – Pap**er** is station**ery**

Surprise – UR surprised

Practice – **C**hoir practi**ce** (noun)

Practise – **S**he practi**se**s her **s**pellings (verb)

Library – **Rar**e books in the lib**rar**y

3 Ask the class if they know any other examples, and invite them to make up mnemonics for words they still find difficult.

I5 Learning by sight

YOU WILL NEED:

▶ OHT I5.1

▶ Handout I5.2, enough for one each

1 Show OHT I5.1 and explain that the two words represented by shapes are words for colours. Write in the first one (gold) as an example, then try to get the class to guess the other (yellow).

2 Distribute handout I5.2 and allow 5 minutes for pupils to come up with words for colours that fit the gaps. Debrief quickly:

1. cream

2. green

3. blue

4. black

5. red

6. brown

7. silver

8. grey

9. purple

10. pink

11. white

12. orange

3 Ask pupils what strategies they employed to match words to shapes. Draw out the importance of registering:

* length

* the position of ascenders and descenders

* overall shape.

4 Ask or suggest to pupils other ways of drawing attention to word shape as an aid to learning. For example:

* highlighter pen over the difficult section

* drawing a close-fitting box around the word

- colour or glitter the word on a sheet of paper then put it where you will see it often, e.g. by bed, on bedroom door, toilet door, end of bath, on mirror, as a screen saver.

16 Learning by sound

YOU WILL NEED:
▶ OHT 16.1

1 Explain that learning by sound is useful for longer words. There are several strategies to help.

2 The first strategy is to break it into syllables. Use 'remember' as your example. Explain that it has three syllables or beats in it, which can be detected by clapping out its parts, e.g. re-mem-ber. Demonstrate this.

3 Show the top list of OHT 16.1 and ask the class to work out the number of syllables in each word. Hint: it is easier to listen to the syllables than to look for them in print. Allow only a minute or so.

4 Clap out the answers:
- be – ginn – ing (3)
- co – op – er – a – tive (5)
- im – pol – ite (2)
- tel – e – phone (3)
- in – ter – est – ed (4)
- in – con – ven – i – ent (5)
- in – ex – tin – guish – ab – le (6)

5 Now show the words in the middle section of the OHT and ask the class to work out the order of the missing letters by sounding out the word in phonemes, attending closely to the order of sounds in each word.
diary
reliant
soliloquy
accident
giant

6 Now show the lower section of the OHT and suggest a third strategy for words containing silent or quiet letters: sound them out as they are spelt. Avoid this strategy if your class contains pupils who are new to English, as it can mislead them about pronunciation.

7 If your class is ready for it, you could look at some more demanding examples where a part of the word is hard to hear because it is unstressed:

- chocolate
- particularly
- interested
- gradually

- eventually
- temporary
- happened.

17 Looking it up

YOU WILL NEED:

▶ Cards I7.1, enough for one set between two

▶ A dictionary for each pupil

1 Distribute dictionaries to each pupil and then ask pupils to find with their finger the middle page and open it. Most dictionaries open around M. Point out how it is useful to remember the letter M at the middle when searching for words in a dictionary.

2 Quick activity: Ask the pupils in which half of the dictionary will the following words be found? Aim, begin, tell, look, mean, become, stream, television, zebra.

3 Move on to quartering the dictionary. Ask pupils to guess which letters will appear when they try the finger exercise again, halving the two sections they have already created.

4 Take suggestions and try it. The first quarter often ends at E and the third quarter often ends at S. Point out that by knowing where these cut-off points are, your search is cut down by three-quarters.

5 Provide a mnemonic to remember the cut-off points: Eggs Make Smells.

6 Distribute the cards, one set between two. Each card represents a particular quarter of the dictionary. Explain that you will read aloud some words and they have to agree which quarter of the dictionary it is in. Read a word and then pause before asking pupils to show a card. This builds in thinking time.

international (2)

tremendous (4)

onomatopoeia (3)

fashion (2)

business (1)

yoghurt (4)

necessary (3)

buddhism (1)

government (2)

religion (3)

7 Point out the value of using the key words at the top of the page. Ask pupils to turn to a particular page in the dictionary, and ask them to put up a hand as soon as they know whether a particular nearby word comes before, on or after the page.

18 Spellchecker tips

YOU WILL NEED:

▶ One hand-held spellchecker for demonstration purposes

▶ A hand-held or computer spellchecker

▶ Dictionaries (one per pupil)

▶ Whiteboards and marker pens

1 Discuss the advantages and disadvantages of using spellcheckers instead of dictionaries.

2 Give the children a simple alphabetical order activity to see who can find the correct spelling quickest, a pupil with a dictionary, or a pupil with a piece of paper and a spellchecker. You may like to choose the words for the pupils to look up, alternatively try these: necessarily, privilege. Choose a tricky word, as there is no point looking up a word they know.

3 Point out that spellcheckers are useful only for looking up the occasional word we cannot spell or have mistyped. To spell-check a whole document that is full of errors takes time and is not completely reliable either. One still has to decide, for example between 'their', 'there'; 'where', 'were' and 'wear'.

4 Game 1: Type the names of towns, villages and people's names and see what alternatives the computer suggests. How does the computer work on spellings? On what basis does it offer alternatives?

5 Game 2: Using spellcheckers.
If you check your spellings on the computer, you will be offered a list of alternative words for every word it cannot recognise. For instance. if you type a misspelling for the word 'salt', the computer tries to help by providing you with these to chose from: 'Celt', 'sell', 'self', 'sells', 'seat' and 'sect'.

Either: make up a poem using some or all of these words in each line.

Or: find five alternative words for each of those provided.

Ask pupils how they should choose from the list of words offered.

6 Spellchecker on the Internet.

For homework, pupils are to find the meanings of the following Internet words; and develop ways to remember them, e.g. acronym; word shape; highlighting syllables; mnemonic; look; cover; say; write and check; etc.

- clickstream
- crash
- cyberspace
- eyeballsearch
- infobahn
- hacking
- smiley
- surfer
- timeout
- virus
- wired.

Section J: Vocabulary

J1 Working out the meaning of unfamiliar words

YOU WILL NEED:

▶ OHT J1.1

1 Tell pupils you are going to show them what some people say is the longest word in the dictionary (though complicated, children find such a word of great interest).

2 Show the word at the top of OHT J1.1 and give pupils a minute or so in pairs to try to work out the meaning.

3 Take suggestions. Most importantly, draw out the strategies pupils use to unpick the word. These will include:

- Break the word down and sound it out.
- Look for words within words.
- Look for analogies.
- Identifying the base word with a fixed meaning – establish which has a fixed meaning.
- Taking account of the prefixes 'anti' and 'dis'.
- Taking account of the suffixes 'ment', 'arian' and 'ism' (-arian may seem difficult, prompt with 'librarian' if necessary).

Use the next section of the OHT to demonstrate how the meaning of the word can be deduced by breaking it into its constituents.

4 Once all elements have been discussed, introduce the idea of context by showing pupils the sentence on the OHT in which the word is used. With your help, they should approach the meaning, which is: wanting to keep tradition, i.e. opposing those who wish to remove the setting up of an established power such as the church or government.

5 Reveal the mystery words at the bottom of the OHT and help pupils to work out the meaning of each one from its parts.

Mystery word	Familiar roots	Analogies
Quadrennial	quad = 4 ennial = yearly	millennium biennial
Chronometer	chrono = time meter = measure	chronology meter
Telethon	tele = distant	marathon decathlon
Exemplification	example ify = verb ation = noun	exemplify magnification

J2 Terms of qualification

YOU WILL NEED:

▶ OHT J2.1

▶ Handout J2.2

1 Show the sentences on OHT J2.1 and ask pupils to discuss for a minute the function of the words in bold.

2 Take feedback and work towards the idea that they all qualify meaning in some way by limiting, specifiying or emphasising meaning. They are useful in writing because they express a degree of subtlety, and show that the writer does not think simply in black and white.

3 Distribute Handout OHT J2.2. and allow pupils 3 to 5 minutes to

a) identify the term of qualification in each of the twelve sentences; and

b) allocate the sentence to the correct box.

4 This can be achieved by cutting up then positioning the sentence strips or by transcribing the number into the correct box:

To exclude or subtract	1
To be more specific or precise	2 4 11
To heighten or emphasise	3 5 12
To lower or limit	6 7 8 9
To add or include	10

J3 Terms of comparison

YOU WILL NEED:

▶ OHT J3.1

1 Remind pupils of the familiar way of making comparisons by adding -ER and -EST. One example is shown on the OHT. Re-introduce the terms comparative and superlative.

2 Ask pupils to tell you which one you should use if you are comparing only two objects e.g. the length of two straws. Look for the response: -ER

3 If necessary, revise the spelling rules which affect vowel suffixes.

4 Now remind the class that not all comparatives are made by adding a suffix. Some, such as beautiful, take 'more' and 'most'. Try asking pupils for other examples of words taking 'more' and 'most' instead of -ER or -EST.

5 Show the rest of the OHT and ask pupils to consider for a minute or 2 whether there is any pattern to the words which use 'more' and 'most' instead of -ER and -EST. Look for the responses:

- Three syllable words take 'more' or 'most'.
- Most words already ending in a suffix 'more' and 'most'.
- Most words ending in Y or LY take -ER and -EST.
- Two syllable words vary in the way they form the comparative.

6 Finally ask the class if they can think of any words which use neither -ER/-EST nor more/most. Look for:

- bad, worse, worst
- good, better, best
- much, more, most
- little, less, least.

It may be of interest to explain that these irregular forms originated in Old English. As with irregular verbs, the most commonly used words have retained their original patterns.

J4 Less or fewer?

YOU WILL NEED:

▶ OHT J4.1

1 Explain directly that the purpose of this starter is to resolve a common confusion between 'less' and 'few'.

2 Show OHT J4,1 and ask pupils to decide whether they should use 'less' or 'fewer' in each case.

3 After a minute, give them the answers and ask them to work out a rule. Look for the reponse:

- 'Less' for singular, when you are dealing with amounts.
- 'Fewer' for plurals, when you are dealing with numbers.

4 Point out that when we speak of 'more', we use the same word so no confusion occurs.

Section K: Link words

K1 Words for comparing and contrasting

AIM: To introduce connectives for comparing and contrasting

YOU WILL NEED:
- ▶ OHT K1.1
- ▶ OHT K1.2
- ▶ Two highlighters pens in different colours

1 Identify the focus of the session as comparing and constrasting, and establish that they understand the difference between comparison and contrast.

2 Give three oral examples, asking them to listen for the linking phrases:
- Terry likes Salt and Vinegar crisps **whereas** Rachel adores Cheese and Onion flavour.
- Terry squeezes his spots **in just the same way** that Rachel squeezes hers.
- Terry could do his homework. **On the other hand**, he could just do nothing.

3 Show OHT K1.1 and ask someone to come out and identify a connective suitable for comparing things, then one for contrasting. Ask for further volunteers and repeat. Hurry things along – this is easy.

4 Turn off the OHT immediately and ask pairs to draw a line down the middle of a page and head one COMPARISON and one CONTRAST. Tell them to list at least 6 words in each column.

5 Take answers, and tell the others to add new words to their lists as they come up. Reward pupils with more than six.

6 Show OHT K1.2 as a back up and make a photocopy to put on the classroom wall. Make sure pupils have a permanent record and remind them of it when you come to argumentative and persuasive writing.

7 Go back to the oral examples you used. Ask pupils: Where in a sentence do link words (usually called connectives if they join ideas within a single sentence) usually occur? The obvious answer is in the middle. But it is by no means the only place. Ask pupils to rephrase the first two sentences so that the connective comes first or last.
e.g.

Although Terry likes Salt and Vinegar crisps, Rachel adores Cheese and Onion flavour.

Terry likes Salt and Vinegar crisps. Rachel adores Cheese and Onion, **however**.

K2 Temporal connectives

AIM:	To introduce words that link events by time and sequence

YOU WILL NEED:

▶ OHT K2.1

1   Remind pupils of the importance of connectives in joining ideas together to make writing flow, and identify time and sequence as the focus of the session.

2   Show the top section of OHT K2.1 but keep the lower section covered. If pupils are familiar with writing frames, tell them that this is what it is. It might be used as a list of prompts to write a recipe or a set of instructions, for example. It could also be used to write a simple story. This is because the prompts are all about time and sequence. They signal to the reader when and in what order something happens.

3   Write up and explain the word *chronological*.

4   Remind pupils that you have mentioned two kinds of writing that are organised by the order in which events happen: instructions and narrative. Ask them if they can suggest specific examples of types of writing arranged in chronological order. Start them off with recipes and fairy tales. Do this orally, e.g. directions, witness statements, explanations, recipes, writing up experiments, repair manuals.

5   Now give groups 2-3 minutes to brainstorm as many connectives as they can which link ideas by signalling time.

6   Take responses orally until the class have exhausted their supply. You may need to field some ambiguous answers such as 'six o' clock' or 'evening' or 'February'. In fact, they can be used as links e.g. 'By evening, Laura had arrived home from work', but pupils sometimes suggest them because they have only vaguely grasped the idea of time. The proper response is to ask them for a sentence in which it is used as a connective to join ideas in a sequence. A true connective will do this.

7   Show the remainder of OHT K2.1 if you need to: the pupil list may have been sufficient.

8   Remind pupils that examiners often complain about the over-use of the link 'then', and that this list should act as a reminder to them of the alternatives.

9   Using the famous fairy tale opening 'Once upon a time', ask pupils to choose a simple nursery rhyme such as *Humpty Dumpty*, *Jack and Jill*, *Little Miss Muffet*, and retell the story, using no connective more than once. Listen to various versions, pointing out original or effective usage.

K3 Causal connectives

AIM: To introduce words that make a link between cause and effect

YOU WILL NEED:
▶ OHT K3.1
▶ OHT K3.2

1 Use the sentences on OHT K3.1 and ask pupils to identify the connecting word or phrase which tells you that one event was caused by another. Circle the connectives. Note that the third sentence contains two connectives. If they don't spot this, simply wait. Say 'Keep looking'.

2 Ask pupils if they can guess which is the most commonly used connective the answer is 'because'. 'Because' is over-used and the point of this session is to suggest alternatives.

3 Ask them to brainstorm alternatives for 2-3 minutes. This might be a good moment to suggest a strategy: Adopt a 'cloze procedure' approach to the sentences on OHT K3.1, thinking of words that would fit in the place of the circled connectives.

4 Take responses and reward pupils who think of several examples. Use OHT K3.2 if you wish, to supplement the pupils' suggestions, and display a copy on the classroom wall. Ask pupils to record the list and ask them to reflect on when they might need them, e.g. in science.

5 Put up OHT K3.1 again and ask pupils which half of the sentence is cause and which is effect. You could highlight them in two different colours. Ask pupils if there is a link between order and the choice of connective?

6 Look for the answer that there is. For example:
- 'therefore' is always preceded by cause and followed by effect
- 'because' is always followed by cause, though the effect can move around.

Ask pupils to generalise about the sequence in:
- 'is caused by' (preceded by effect, followed by cause)
- 'consequently' (preceded by cause and followed by effect)
- 'as a result of' (is always followed by cause though the effects can move around).

Establish that some links dictate their position in sentences.

K4 Connectives for adding and summating

| **AIM**: | To introduce connectives which add and summate |

YOU WILL NEED:

▶ K4.1 as an OHT and enough copies for one between two
▶ OHT K4.2

1 Have OHT K4.1 ready and photocopies already on the desks (one per pair).

2 Explain the aim of the session and show OHT K4.1. On the OHT, begin by circling the first two connectives which express addition or increase. Stop at this point and ask pupils to continue on their sheets to find at least six more examples.

> Becoming a good cook has a number of advantages. It improves your social life: everyone loves a good meal with great company, **and** everyone likes it when someone else does the cooking! It is **also** an opportunity to relax over a pastime that is appreciated by others. **Furthermore** there may be a career in it: you could become one of the rising number of celebrity television chefs!
>
> There are, however, some important drawbacks. Think of the time spent preparing food **and** clearing up **as well as** waiting by the cooker. **In addition**, you should consider the time taken shopping for ingredients, **and** also the financial cost **and** plain hard work of serious cooking.
>
> Chefs are agreed that, <u>taking all the factors into consideration</u>, the wise cook buys a dishwasher **and also** makes the family help with the preparation **and** clearing. <u>Overall</u>, cooking has its drawbacks, but the results are worth it.

3 Take feedback and circle them as you go. (Bold above).

4 Next ask pupils to find two examples of connectives – either words or phrases – which don't *add* but *sum* up. (Underlined above).

5 Ask pupils if they can think of any other words or phrases that could be used to summate. (For your information see OHT K4.2).

6 Put pupils into small groups and challenge them to brainstorm in two lists as many *adding* and *summating* connectives as they can think of. Praise substantial lists.

7 Use OHT K4.2 to debrief if necessary, and use it for classroom display.

K5 Words for use in argument 1

AIM: To introduce connectives for presenting arguments

YOU WILL NEED:

▶ Cards K5.1, enough for one set between two

1 Have the word cards already cut, in envelopes and distributed between twos or threes at the most.

2 IMPORTANT: In introducing the aim of the session, do not reveal the type of connectives in the title. Just say you are continuing to look at connectives. Remind pupils of the types of connectives already considered, as this will get them thinking at the right level of generality for the next step.

3 Ask pupils to empty the envelopes and work out what type of connectives they are and where one might find them. Look for the response: In argument, setting out a case or an opinion.

4 Ask pupils if they can group and classify the words by purpose. As an example, pick out the word *certainly* and ask pupils what the purpose of it is in the context of presenting an opinion. Look for the response: It assures or confirms a view, it urges the reader to accept that an idea is right. Ask pupils to find other words that do the same job and group them together.

5 Take feedback from groups. Some of the classifications will overlap, but that doesn't matter. Look for:
   • Qualifying – despite, although, unless, assuming – which qualify or modify an idea that has been expressed
   • Assurances – certainly, clearly, obviously
   • Causal – because, therefore, and so
   • Comparing and contrasting – on the other hand, whereas
   • Summarising – in conclusion, overall
   • Adding – furthermore, moreover
   • Exemplifying – for example, for instance
   • Emphasising – indeed, most of all, absolutely.

6 Note that this theme is continued in the next starter.

K6 Words for use in argument 2

AIM:	To memorise some words for use in argument

YOU WILL NEED;

▶ Cards K5.1 used in the last session, enough for one set between two

▶ Handout K6.1, enough for one between two at first, but enough for one each later

1 Have the handouts of K6.1 and the word cards ready on the desk for use by pairs.

2 Remind pupils of the classification of words in the last few starters. These are featured in the headings on the sheet.

3 Ask pupils to place word cards in the correct boxes. Circulate to check these are generally correct.

4 Quickly allocate groups with responsibility for each classification.

5 Give a provocative topic such as *Each year group should wear a different colour sweatshirt* or something amusing such as *Pupils should be allowed to bring their pets to school*. Ask each group to think of a sentence in this argument that might call for a connective from their list. Encourage them to make you laugh, e.g.

- *Certainly*, Y9 deserve sludge-coloured sweatshirts.
- Whippets, *for example*, would be a useful addition to the sports curriculum.
- *Surely* no-one would deny the right of hamsters to learn French?

6 Tell pupils to pack away the word cards and collect them in.

7 Distribute the other blank K6.1 sheets so that each pupil has their own copy and ask them to write as many examples as they can recall into the boxes. Tell them to store this sheet for use when they come to write argument.

K7 Creative thinking

AIM:	To introduce vocabulary prompts that can aid creative thinking

YOU WILL NEED:

▶ OHT K7.1

1 Explain the aim of the lesson and show the top section of OHT K7.1. Ask them to think about any one of the propositions for 2 minutes.

2 Take a couple of examples and ask them what they did in their own mind. If this is hard, you could model this by revealing the process you went through: 'At first I imagined swimming underwater looking at the fish and plants, then I thought about having gills and how horrible that would be. Then I wondered if I could still breathe in the air, and imagined choking. I thought I might go to the landside for my holiday.'

Draw out the kind of thing we do when we imagine situations – we visualise, act out, ask questions, compare it with what we do now, pursue consequences.

3   Ask pupils which words in the questions prompted them to do this. Look for the boldfaced words.

What if people could fly?

Suppose we could read other people's minds.

Imagine you could breathe under water.

Maybe you will live forever.

What if we could speak every language in the world?

Perhaps you will marry someone you already know.

Point out that two of them are instructions (imagine, suppose) which pupils obediently followed. But what are the others? Look for:

- **hypothetical questions** which invite the reader to speculate – *what if...?*
- **conditional** words – *maybe, perhaps* which play with an idea but don't commit to it. It could happen, but it may not.

4   Explain that these are invitations to **speculate** – another word for imagining or playing with ideas. All powerful learners can speculate.

5   Reveal the lower half of the OHT and ask pupils to brainstorm for two minutes, words that might go in each list. Pool ideas and write them up. Look for:

Questions	Conditionals	Instructions
What if...?	Maybe...	Imagine...
Why might...?	Perhaps...	Pretend...
How might...?	Possibly...	Consider...
When might...?	Probably...	Suppose...
Who might...?	Perhaps...	Assume...
If..., then...?	Could...	Predict...
	Would...	
	Might...	
	Presumably...	

6 Ask pupils to give you an example of how phrases might come in handy in:

- making a difficult decision
- working out why something happened
- trying to get at someone to change their mind
- responding to an unrealistic suggestion
- helping your reader to see what the benefits of a proposal might be
- testing an idea to see if it's always true.

7 Ask pupils to record the words in the columns and remind them to draw on these lists when they come to write speculatively. On this occasion, you should also remind them that they have learnt an important thinking tool. They can use these words on themselves to unpack ideas and think through problems.

Section L: Language variation

L1   Words borrowed from other languages

YOU WILL NEED:
- ▶ OHT L1.1
- ▶ Handout L1.2, enough for one between two

1   Show the first set of words on the OHT and ask pupils what they have in common. Look for the response: They are all borrowed from the French.

2   Ask pupils if they can think of more French phrases we use in everyday language, e.g. 'en route', 'cul de sac', 'grand prix'.

3   Remind pupils that this process is two-way. Do they know of any English phrases that have found their way into the French language? For example, 'le weekend', 'le camping', 'le sandwich', 'le football'.

4   Ask if they can explain how French came to be such a common source of English words. Look for responses including proximity, trade, settlers, the fact that England was ruled by the French (after the Battle of Hastings).

5   Develop the last point to say that the English language has been shaped by different languages used by invaders. It is almost 1000 years since England was invaded, but the language still reflects their influence. Who were they? Look for the answers: Romans, Angles, Jutes, Vikings.

6   Reveal the word 'Telephone' in the middle section of the OHT, and ask if this word has been borrowed. It is obviously a new word, because telephones are a recent invention. It was coined by using classical Greek words (tele = distant, phone = hear).

7   Now show the list of foods and drinks. Explain that foods and drinks are quickly exported and their names come with them. In the days of air travel and preservatives, there has been a boom in international cuisine. Food words travel quickly. Ask pupils to identify which countries they come from, and how the spelling of words reflect this, e.g. the 'I' ending on pasta dishes is borrowed from the Italian plural.

Champagne – French (a region)

Port – Portuguese after the city of Oporto

Sherry – Spanish after the city Jerez

Vodka – Russian

Pizza – Italian

Risotto – Italian

Spaghetti – Italian

Vermicelli – Italian
Tortillas – Spanish
Fajitas – Spanish
Bhaji – Indian
Crème fraiche – French
Kebab – Arabic

8 Distribute Handout L1.2 and ask pupils in pairs to match the words to the languages *without* dictionaries. The answers are below:

1.	America	movie
2.	America	motel
3.	Arabic	algebra
4.	Arabic	sherbet
5.	Arabic	zero
6.	Australia	didgeridoo
7.	Australia	boomerang
8.	China	tea
9.	Eskimo	igloo
10.	Germany	kindergarten
11.	Germany	blitz
12.	India	pyjamas
13.	Israel	kibbutz
14.	Italy	balcony
15.	Italy	carnival
16.	Italy	casino
17.	Italy	gondola
18.	Jamaica	reggae
19.	Japan	kimono
20.	Malaya	bamboo
21.	Mexico	chocolate
22.	Persia	caravan
23.	Spain	siesta
24.	Spain	matador

L2 Words with close relatives in other languages

YOU WILL NEED:

▶ OHT L2.1

1 Show the first group of words on OHT L2.1 and ask if they can work out the English word that matches these. Look for the response: Brother.

2 Explain that many English words have similarities with their equivalents in European and Asian languages. This is because they were derived from the same source. Explain that language experts believe that a language known as Indo-European was the source of all modern European languages. As people spread across Asia and Europe, they took this language with them, but they also began to develop it, adding new local words and ways of expressing ideas. This is how new languages develop, and continue to change. The words which have survived with little change tend to be those most used and most important such as the words we use for family relationships, parts of the body, domestic animals and weather conditions.

3 Show the other groups of words and ask pupils to work out the English equivalents, by drawing analogies with English words which are closely related.

- family
- school
- wife (using the link with feminine)
- horse (using the link with cavalry).

4 Ask pupils to suggest other words that they know from other languages which are similar to the English.

L3 American vocabulary and spelling

YOU WILL NEED:

▶ OHT L3.1

1 Show the words at the top of OHT L3.1 and ask pupils how they are typical of American spellings. Look for the answer:

- OUR endings are spelt OR
- French feminine endings, e.g. MME, are reduced to M.

2 Show the main list of words and go through them, seeking the English equivalents. The answers are given overleaf.

USA	UK
sidewalk	*pavement*
elevator	*lift*
purse	*handbag*
gas	*petrol*
frosting	*icing*
vest	*waist-coat*
Hi!	*hello*
zucchini	*courgette*
sweater	*jumper*
suspenders	*braces*
candy	*sweets*

USA	UK
jelly	*jam*
garbage	*rubbish*
firecrackers	*fireworks*
pants	*trousers*
fall	*Autumn*
ladybug	*ladybird*
cookies	*biscuits*
faucet	*tap*
french fries	*chips*
thumb tack	*drawing pin*
check	*bill*

3 Ask pupils if they can explain the separate development of vocabulary in an English-speaking country, and how they come to know these alternatives themselves. You could mention that:

- American ancestors came from Britain and retained some words that have changed in England. Some words found in Shakespeare (around the time of the first emigrations to America) are still current in America (e.g. gotten, fall, platter, trash, skillet).

- American TV programmes, computer software and the internet have made American vocabulary familiar to English ears.

- Other languages have contributed to American English also, e.g.
  Dutch: yankee
  Spanish: rodeo, rancher
  French: prairie, dime
  Indian: canoe, tobacco.

L4 Changing language

YOU WILL NEED:

▶ OHT L4.1

▶ Cards L4.2

1 Show the first set of lines on OHT L4.1 and ask pupils if they can work out what they mean before you show them the next two versions. The three pairs of lines show how language has changed over the last 1000 years, starting with the Anglo-Saxon version of the Lord's prayer, then the

St James bible of the 17th century and the modern day equivalent.

2   Establish that language is always evolving, with some words dying out and others being added or changing.

3   Distribute cards made from L4.2 and ask pupils to organise the appropriate words under the capitalised headings. Allow 3 minutes.

4   After 3 minutes, discuss their decisions, exploring what meanings they are attributing to the words and phrases.

Words which are going out of date:

Frock   wireless   luncheon   commercial traveller

Words which are changing in meaning:

gay   wicked   alien   virus

Words which reflect fashion in clothes

trainer   tights   tank top   separates

Words which have recently been invented

yuppie   wrinklie   cyberspace   fanzine

Words which reflect new discoveries

transistor   lunar probe   videotape   search engines

5   Ask pupils to suggest other words which are falling out of use or coming into use.

L5 Meanings and context

YOU WILL NEED:

▶ OHT L5.1

1   Show the four words at the top of OHT L5.1 and ask pupils in each case what they might write next to them if they were composing a dictionary entry for the word. Allow 4 minutes.

2   Take feedback and reward concise answers and draw out the number of different meanings held in each word.

3   Show the first definition for 'window' and ask the pupils to predict the word it is defining. Take suggestions without comment and then show the next definition, which will confirm 'window' as the correct answer. Finally show the third example which demonstrates a metaphorical use of the word. This extract was taken from a NASA transcript about a lunar expedition.

4   Now reveal the other words which have particular uses in school subjects but general uses outside of school. Ask pupils to define both.

L6 Definitions

YOU WILL NEED:

▶ Handout L6.1

▶ Dictionary per pair

1 Ask pupils in groups to brainstorm the different meanings of the word 'round'.

2 Once you have drawn out several definitions, ask pupils how many different word classes the word 'round' can be used in.

3 Ask them to check this in the dictionary, showing them how word classes are signposted in your class dictionaries.

4 Whilst the dictionaries are out, walk them through some of the features of the definitions, which may include:

- Parts of speech are identified, possibly more than once if a word can have different functions.
- Guide to pronunciation.
- Meanings.
- Such meanings are numbered with the most common meaning coming first.
- A brief example of each different use of the word is supplied.
- Special phrases or compounds may be covered at the end of the definition.
- The origin of the word is given either at the beginning or end of the definition.

5 Now set a challenge to the class using Handout L6.1 to provide the different uses and word classes of the following words:

Test

Beat

Book

Form

Heat

Section A: Vowels

A1.1 Long A (1)

Short A	Long A
hat	hate
clam	claim
plan	play
past	paste

apple	essay	blame	human
Santa	main	cat	jacket
carrot	rabbit	band	baby
face	stand	pain	match
vein	rain	rein	reign
act	sail	ale	play
stay	anchor	ant	bank
track	pray		

Long A (2)

tame	mane	sail	raid
delay	stale	fate	made
rail	grade	claim	cake
fame	train	say	lace
cage	explain	ace	fade
gain	maid	dismay	shape
shame	main	race	rate
sway	maiden	chase	inflate
same	blame	taste	mate
debate	pain	display	scale
dame	bray	baste	stage
day	waist	array	rage
sane	rain	haste	pay
pane	brain	waste	today
crane	paint	face	lay
plane	pail	grace	tray
play	spray	cape	place
pale	grail	gaze	essay

A2.2 Long A (2)

1 What is the most common way of making the long A sound?

2 AY usually appears where?

3 How to do you choose between A-E and AI?

Long E

Short E	Long E
edit	week
message	treat
strength	relief
sent	ceiling
devil	demon
health	even

feet   rent   beggar

delete   best   dress

reason   conceive   pedal

	Beginning	Middle	End
ee			
ea			
ei			
e-e			
ie			
e-other vowel			

A8.1 OY and OI

toy	oil
joy	toil
boy	soil
enjoy	boil
destroy	noisy
annoy	joint
coy	pointed
employ	voice
enjoyment	coin
employed	moist
annoyance	toilet
joyful	turmoil
oyster	poison
royal	choice
loyal	
voyage	

OY or OI

OY	OI
OY	OI
OY	OI
OY	OI
OY	OI
OY	OI

A9.1 AIR, ARE, EAR, ERE and EIR

AIR	ARE	EAR	ERE	EIR

AW and AU

saw	fraught	applause
maw	caught	gawp
dawn	awe	flaw
audit	saucer	audition
awkward	paucity	draw
claw	paw	drawn
author	bauble	drawer
brawny	audible	fault
sawn	fawn	haunt
naught	auditory	audience
laundry	pawn	haul
raw	auditorium	awful
shawl	launch	awesome
straw	raunchy	lawn
naughty	jaw	crawl

A12.1 IE and EI

piece	sieve	friend
believe	priest	mischief
fierce	chief	pierce
shriek	cashier	thief
review	niece	shield
obedient	ancient	patient
science	conscience	quiet

IE and EI continued

die	diet	grief
relief	tie	lie
either	reign	rein
perceive	receive	vein
deceive	freight	neighbour
conceit	neither	weird

A12.1 IE and EI continued

protein	their	eight
foreign	leisure	weight
ceiling	sovereign	height
medieval	siege	brief
hygiene	ingredient	beige
pie	eiderdown	

IE and EI

1   Which is the most common choice – IE or EI?

2   Which is commonly used at the end of words?

3   Which is commonly used at the beginning of words?

4   Which one often sounds like long A (the sound in the word DAY)?

5   Which one usually comes after C?

6   Can you spot a pattern in the exceptions to the C rule?

7   Which is used if GN comes after? And what meaning do these words share?

A12.3 IE and EI

ie ei

Vowel and double consonants

diner	dinner
writing	written
biter	bitten
rider	ridden
hide	hidden
coma	comma

A13.2 Vowels and double consonants

rip	ripple
mud	muddle
pop	popped
bite	biting
run	running
rip	ripping
stop	stopped
decide	deciding
mop	mopping
make	making
refer	referring
skip	skipping
hop	hopped
jog	jogging
hug	hugged
drive	driving

Softening C

List 1	List 2
cuddle	decide
discuss	cereal
uncle	cinema
traffic	descend
calendar	recite
picnic	notice
camera	cycle
curtain	fancy
carnival	graceful

A14.2 Softening C

cyclist	noticeable	cylinder
advance	circulation	certain
celebrate	accident	mercy
incident	ceremony	recent
circuit	service	decisive
process	spicy	incense
decimal	citizen	success
civil	decent	sequence

Softening G

List 1	List 2
bag	gerbil
guess	imagine
drag	danger
goldfish	village
jog	magic
goat	gym
gable	giant
gape	large
agate	Egypt

A15.2 Softening G

geranium	emergency	bridge
stranger	energy	engine
damage	grudge	gymnasium
imagine	fringe	legend
ginger	gymnastics	obliged
gypsy	generous	management
giraffe	gym	geometry
suggest	ridge	gibbet
gyrate	ledge	language
gender	gyroscope	giant
general	voyage	dredge
merge	genuine	encourage
gibberish	tinge	gymkhana

Hard-to-hear vowels (1)

interest	business
family	corporal
factory	different
lettuce	parliament
original	doctor
definite	separate
geography	history
primary	carpet

A16.2 Hard-to-hear vowels (1)

Saturday	familiar
alcohol	sector
description	television
predict	company
miniature	illiterate
guard	lemonade
freedom	vegetable
category	similar
definite	miserable
hospital	astronomy
poisonous	holiday
stationary	describe
medicine	animal
lottery	prepare
abandoned	separate
centre	messenger
prosperous	margarine

Hard-to-hear vowels (2)

fattening	smuggler
dandelion	generous
conference	widening
consonant	similar
lottery	memorable
prosperous	stationery
voluntary	different
abominable	library
history	lettuce
marvellous	factory
miserable	extra
jewellery	literate
heaven	difference
signature	frightening
flattery	illiterate
parallel	interest
dictionary	secretary
vegetable	mathematics
category	explanatory
interested	messenger
deepening	desperate

A18.1 Revision

1   What is the difference between short vowels and long vowels?

    _____

2   Circle the most common ways to spell the long A:
    AI   AY   A-E

3   Choose between AI and AY in these words:

    barg__n   displ__   pr__er   st__n

4   Write down the three most common ways of spelling the long E sound, and
    give an example of each.

    _____
    _____
    _____

5   Circle the correct spelling:
    delete   deleet   deleat

6   IE or EI? Insert the correct letters.

    bel__ve   rec__ve   misch__f   v__n   for__gn   c__ling

7   Write two words containing the long U which do not use the
    letter U at all. Two points if you use two different ways to spell long U.

    _____   _____

8   Insert OI/OY correctly:

    p__sonous   env__   destr__   v__d

9   Fill in the quiet vowels in the following words:
    int__rest   hist__ry   defin__te   sep__rate   diff__rent   bus__ness

10 Why is there only one T in **writing** but two in **written**?

    _____

11 Fill in double or single consonants:
    Eating di__er.   Bees carry po__en.

12 Spell correctly five words you get wrong in the work on vowels. Ask a
    partner to test you and write here:

    _____ _____ _____ _____ _____

Section B: Plurals

B1.1 ES Plurals

A	B	C
teams	games	fishes
cars	fires	churches
shops	clues	witches
meals	tables	hisses
rooms	crates	buses
chairs	whales	foxes
books	cages	wishes

ES plurals

s | es

B2.1 Plurals for words ending in Y

YS	
boy	boys
alloy	alloys
play	plays
alley	alleys
monkey	monkeys
day	days

IES	
party	parties
jury	juries
luxury	luxuries
robbery	robberies
battery	batteries
spy	spies

Plurals for words ending in Y

B2.2

singular	plural	singular	plural
country		body	
boy		storey	
query		laboratory	
donkey		treaty	
try		story	
redundancy		century	
journey		emergency	
city		fantasy	
subsidy		chimney	
decoy		osprey	
valley		currency	
vacancy		diary	
dictionary		quay	
delay		birthday	
key		savoury	
loyalty		array	
memory		photocopy	
history		galaxy	
display		accessory	

B3.1 **Plurals for words ending in F**

stuff ⟶ stuffs

handcuff ⟶ handcuffs

calf ⟶ calves

half ⟶ halves

loaf ⟶ loaves

leaf ⟶ leaves

knife ⟶ knives

life ⟶ lives

Plurals for words ending in F

fs   ves

B4.1 Plurals for words ending in vowels

+S		+ES	
dahlia	dahlias	echo	echoes
concerto	concertos	volcano	volcanoes
gecko	geckos	potato	potatoes
rota	rotas	tomato	tomatoes
piano	pianos	torpedo	torpedoes
zoo	zoos	mosquito	mosquitoes
pizza	pizzas	hero	heroes
yoyo	yoyos		
visa	visas		
puma	pumas		
magnolia	magnolias		
guru	gurus		
banjo	banjos		
radio	radios		
trio	trios		
aria	arias		
pagoda	pagodas		
memo	memos		
banana	bananas		
cuckoo	cuckoos		
mango	mangos		
ski	skis		

Unusual plurals

plateau plateaux	gateau gateaux	die dice
goose geese	foot feet	louse lice
tooth teeth	mouse mice	brother brethren
child children	man men	woman women
antenna antennae	formula formulae	agenda agendae
ox oxen	sheep sheep	matrix matrices
vortex vortices	axis axes	focus foci
penny pence	deer deer	salmon salmon
trout trout	phenomenon phenomena	fungus fungi
cactus cacti	analysis analyses	memorandum memoranda
appendix appendices	oasis oases	chateau chateaux
erratum errata	stratum strata	radius radii
larva larvae	basis bases	crisis crises
hypothesis hypotheses	stimulus stimuli	parenthesis parentheses

B6.1 Revision

1   When should you add an ES to make a plural?

   _____

2   Add S or ES to the following words to make the plural:
   bench__   window__   box__
   kiss__   dish__   school__

3   When should you change the Y to IES to make a plural?

   _____

4   Fill in the plurals of the following words ending in Y:
   journey – _____   holiday   – _____
   country – _____   dictionary – _____
   essay   – _____   baby   – _____

5   Fill in the correct plurals for the following words ending in F:
   wife   – _____   handcuff – _____
   scarf – _____   shelf   – _____

6   Provide two plurals ending in Fs:

   _____   _____

7   Circle the most common plural ending for a word ending in a vowel:
           S   ES

8   Complete the plural form of the following words which end with
   a vowel:
   radio   – _____   tomato   – _____
   volcano – _____   concerto – _____

9   Some words have unusual plurals. Write the plurals for the following:
   axis   – _____   plateau – _____
   cactus – _____   die   – _____

10 Give plurals for:
   party – _____   antenna – _____
   church – _____   donkey – _____
   wife   – _____   crisis – _____
   fly   – _____   cliff   – _____

Section C: Suffixes

C1.1 Suffixes which change the grammatical function of a word 1

Brotherhood Boyhood Neighbourhood	Liquidise Apologise Energise
Beautiful Sinful Helpful	Sadness Kindness Happiness
Technology Biology Geology	Glorify Solidify Signify

Suffixes which change the grammatical function of a word 1

Turn these verbs into nouns:

build	love
paint	hate
sing	push
grow	

Turn these nouns into verbs:

critic	class
summary	anger
sympathy	real
example	

Turn these adjectives into verbs and nouns:

royal	soft
tired	anxious
neutral	clean
warm	

C2.1 Suffixes which change the grammatical function of a word 2

Nouns

-er	-or	-ence	-ism	-ology
-hood	-dom	-ship	-ness	-tion
-age	-ment	-ity	-ery	-ness

Verbs

-ise	-fy	-ate	-en	-er

Adjectives

-est	-er	-some	-less	-ful
-ic	-ive	-ent	-tious	-al
-ish	-able	-ible	-en	-y
-like	-wise			

Adverbs

-ly				

Occupations 1

farmer	instructor
teacher	advisor
worker	operator
builder	director
keeper	administrator
painter	decorator
singer	inspector
waiter	proprietor
grocer	dictator
carpenter	supervisor
gardener	mentor

SHUN endings 1

extension
education
passion

SION endings

extension
explosion
corrosion
division
conclusion

television
confusion
revision
fusion

profession
impression
depression
passion
omission

SHUN endings 2

magician

physician

obstetrician

optician

beautician

clinician

paediatrician

politician

musician

statistician

C7.1 Consonant suffixes

-less
-ful
-ness
-dom
-ship
-like
-hood

---

kind
king
friend

hope
care
shame

lonely
beauty
pity

boy
play
enjoy

Vowel suffixes

-er
-ing
-ed
-ish

Words ending in consonant:
    kind
    king
    friend

Words ending in E:
    hope
    care
    shame

Words ending in consonant + Y:
    lonely
    beauty
    pity

Words ending vowel + Y:
    boy
    play
    enjoy

C10.1 Modifying words ending in Y

List 1	List 2
play ↓ playful	duty ↓ dutiful
coy ↓ coyness	happy ↓ happiness
obey ↓ obeyed	supply ↓ supplied
joy ↓ joyless	penny ↓ penniless

Modifying words ending in Y

play

happy

heavy

apply

rely

enjoy

pity

empty

plenty

holy

boy

way

supply

speedy

C11.1 Changing letters

evoke
provoke

wolf
knife
loaf

decide
extend
erode

panic
frolic
picnic

receive

curious
generous

Able or ible 1

ABLE	IBLE
predictable	edible
drinkable	horrible
reliable	terrible
manageable	impossible
noticeable	visible
readable	audible

oht

C12.2 Able or ible 1

Flashcards – photocopy onto card and cut up

-able	-ible
-able	-ible
-able	-ible
-able	-ible
-able	-ible

long vowels

PLURAL ENDINGS

families *suffixes*

long vowels

prefixes

SUFFIXES

link words

Able or ible 2

Impossible	Noticeable
Probable	Manageable
Knowledgeable	Horrible
Terrible	Possible
Accessible	Responsible
Edible	Possible
Adaptable	Payable
Disposable	Recyclable
Gullible	Fallible
Laughable	Bearable
Enviable	Visible
Sensible	Copiable

C14.1 Cede, ceed, sede and seed endings

Word cards

super	sede	suc	ceed
pro	ceed	ex	ceed
pre	cede	re	cede
lin	seed	bird	seed
ani	seed	ac	cede
inter	cede	con	cede

Definition cards

This ending is used by only one word in the English language.	This ending means *go* or *give way*.
This ending is a word in its own right. It means *germ or growth cell*.	This ending means *go beyond*.

IC endings

magic	magician
physics	physician
music	musician
politics	politician
optics	optician
obstetrics	obstetrician
clinic	clinician

C16.1 L endings 1

wriggle	spectacle	probable	magical	tunnel
snuggle	trickle	drinkable	identical	flannel
kettle	gristle	taxable	medical	channel
paddle	thistle	reliable	practical	cartel
saddle	muscle	presentable	physical	propel
puddle	trestle	amiable	anatomical	cancel
struggle	castle	horrible	personal	camel
bottle	jingle	terrible	exceptional	rebel
skittle	angle	edible	national	panel
shuttle	handle	possible	additional	hotel
dribble	trifle	accessible	seasonal	motel
fiddle	crumble	responsible	traditional	bagel

L endings 1

- Which ending is the most common?

- Which ending is most often used after double letters?

- Which endings are part of common suffixes?

- Which ending follows a recognisable base word?

- Which ending is used for words that clearly rhyme with HELL?

Section D: Prefixes

D1.1 Adding prefixes

dis + appear =

dis + satisfied =

dis + obey =

pre + fix =

pre + face =

pre + empt =

re + play =

re + vise =

re + educate =

Adding prefixes

scopic re	build de	face pre	fix in
active dis	obey non	sense im	possible il
legal anti	clockwise mis	fire contra	vene un
happy ex	change bi	cycle auto	biography tele
sales trans	Atlantic pro	test sub	way micro

D3.1 Number prefixes

bicycle

tricycle

octopus

Octavius Caesar

triceratops

millenium

Number prefixes

Prefix	Number	Examples
uni		
mono		
bi		
duo		
tri		
quad		
pent		
sept		
oct		
dec		
cent		
mill		

D4.1 Latin prefixes

act

actor

action

sense

sensation

sensible

territory

terrace

terrestrial

Latin prefixes

Prefix	Word 1	Word 2	Word 3	Meaning
aqua				
audi				
cap				
dent				
grat				
liber				
lum				
man				
mari				
mem				
min				
mot				
multi				
nov				
ped				
sign				
sta				
tempo				
vac				

Section E: Root words

E1.1 Root words

Root	Word 1	Word 2	Word 3	Meaning
Form	uniform	formation	transform	
Spec	inspect	spectacles	suspect	
Port	import	export	portable	
Circ	circle	circumference	circus	

Root words

geography

geometry

biopsy   geology

biology

antibiotic   astrology

E3.1 # Common roots

Root	Word 1	Word 2	Word 3	Meaning
Mobil				
Sect				
Spir				

Common roots

Root	Word 1	Word 2	Word 3	Meaning
dict				
ten				
text				
tract				
vit				
void				
volv				

E4.1 The spelling of roots

flexible

reflect

reflex

deflect

judge

judicial

prejudice

just

video

evidence

vision

visual

The spelling of roots

Root	Meaning	Word 1	Word 2	Word 3	Word 4
mit/mis	send				
pel/pul	drive				
pens/pend	hang				
cur/cour	run				
voc/voic/vok	call				
ped/pod	foot				
scrib/scrip	write				

Section F: Apostrophes

F1.1 The omission apostrophe

Full Form	Contraction
do not	don't
cannot	can't
is not	isn't
does not	doesn't
will not	won't
shall not	shan't
I had	I'd
I would	I'd
I have	I've
I will	I'll
I am	I'm
are not	aren't
had not	hadn't
have not	haven't
could not	couldn't
could have	could've
would have	would've
should have	should've
mix and match	mix 'n' match
pick and mix	pick 'n' mix
salt and vinegar	salt 'n' vinegar

The possessive apostrophe

My brother's car

- Joes Cafe

- Marys Pantry

- Petes Garage

- Birminghams Great Attraction.

- Englands first team.

The rabbit belongs to Sam.

The book belongs to Tim.

The car belongs to Mr. Anscombe.

The scooter belongs to the boy.

The house belongs to my uncle.

F3.1 Its and it's

- It's been a cold night.

- It's colder than yesterday.

- It's been a year since I saw him.

- It's going to be a close finish.

- It's a good job we came prepared.

- Look carefully at the insect and you'll see it's still alive.

- We found treasure where it's been buried for hundreds of years.

- The dog ran away. It's been missing for days.

- It's a wonder that anyone survived the storm.

- We sheltered where it's safe.

Its and it's

its | it's

F4.1

- Six boys' caps.

- The players' contracts.

- The pupils' books.

_____

Women's fashions

_____

The ladies' coats

The lady's coats

The pupil's work

The pupils' work

Section G: Homophones

G1.1 Homophones

How many socks in a pair?

None, because you eat a pear.

Bare, bear

Air, heir, hair

Where, wear

Homophones

- air, heir,
- bare, bear
- berry, bury
- capital, capitol
- cent, scent, sent
- cite, sight, site
- creak, creek
- ewe, yew, you
- flea, flee,
- foul, fowl
- groan, grown
- here, hear
- hole, whole
- know, no
- base, bass
- blew, blue
- bread, bread
- ceiling, sealing
- cereal, serial
- coarse, course
- currant, current

- fair, fare
- flour, flower
- gnu, knew, new
- hare, hair
- heard, herd
- hour, our
- lead, led
- ate, eight
- be, bee
- bow, bough
- by, buy, bye
- cell, sell
- cheap, cheep
- counsel, council
- earn, urn
- fir, fur
- fore, four, fore
- grate, great
- heal, heel, he'll
- meet, meat
- practise, practice

G2.1 Too, two and to

- It was ____ early.

- He wanted ____ go home.

- She bought ____ tomato pizzas.

Too, two and to

two

too

to

G3.1 Common homophones

rein
rain
reign ☐

you
yew
ewe ☐

rode
road
rowed ☐

to
two
too ☐

by
buy
bye ☐

their
they're
there ☐

sew
so
sow ☐

cent
scent
sent ☐

cell
sell ☐

made
maid ☐

cereal
serial ☐

dear
deer ☐

main
mane ☐

key
quay ☐

beach
beech ☐

meet
meat ☐

scene
seen ☐

blue
blew ☐

pane
pain ☐

vain
vein ☐

Grate
great ☐

peace
piece ☐

waist
waste ☐

hair
hare ☐

plane
plain ☐

fate
fete ☐

here
hear ☐

sum
some ☐

flour
flower ☐

herd
heard ☐

read
red ☐

bean
been ☐

him
hymn ☐

right
write ☐

week
weak ☐

Hour
our ☐

break
brake ☐

leak
leek ☐

knight
night ☐

steel
steal ☐

aloud
allowed ☐

knot
not ☐

stair
stare ☐

board
bored ☐

know
no ☐

tail
tale ☐

sun
son ☐

Common homophones

G3.2

Homophone	Mnemonic

Section H: Unusual word families

H1.1 **Oug and ought**

tough	thought	enough	ought
through	though	cough	although
trough	thorough	drought	sought
plough	rough		

Quiet consonants

Wednesday

Raspberry

Muscle

Design

Cupboard

Christmas

Handbag

KN – knee

WR – wrong

GN – gnome

MB – lamb

SW – answer

ST – castle

PS – psychology

GH – gherkin

GN – sign

SC – science

H3.2 Quiet consonants

lis_en

mor_gage

_sychiatrist

s_ord

stren_th

len_th

su_prise

autum_

su_tle

lib_ary

Feb_uary

gover_ment

enviro_ment

hym_

play_right

dis_ipline

Unusual consonant digraphs 1

ch	kn
gn	th
sh	mb

H4.2 Unusual consonant digraphs 1

Spinners

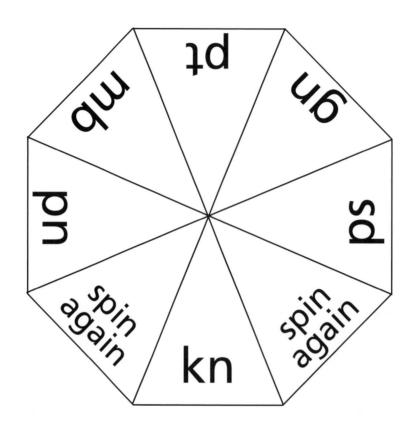

Unusual consonant digraphs

Kn	Ps	Gn

Pt	Mb	Pn

H5.1 Unusual consonant digraphs 2

Across
1 Paper enclosing a sweet or chocolate
3 Flowers or leaves strung together into a ring
4 A sunken ship. To destroy.
6 A deep fold in the skin.
9 Very unfortunate or miserable person.
11 Put down in writing.
12 Joint between hand and arm.
13 A very small bird.
14 Twist like a snake.

Down
2 Not right.
4 To cover a present with paper.
5 Great anger.
7 Struggle to throw someone down.
8 Twist in pain.
10 Squeeze out water by twisting.

Section I: Learning strategies

I2.1 Referring to related words

sign
signature
signal

The lady gave the SIGNAL to SIGN the letter with my SIGNATURE.

---

mus<u>c</u>le
medi<u>c</u>ine
defin<u>it</u>e
th<u>ere</u>
h<u>ea</u>rd
bom<u>b</u>

Words within words

heard
there

---

vegetable

---

knowledge
separate
business
library
island
environment
parliament
definite
immediate
piece
temperature

14.1 Mnemonics

February

Necessary

Friend

Stationary

Stationery

Surprise

Practice

Practise

Library

Learning by sight

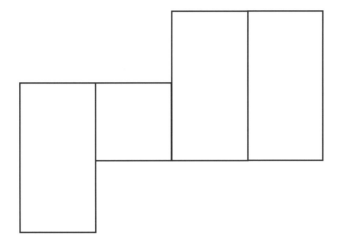

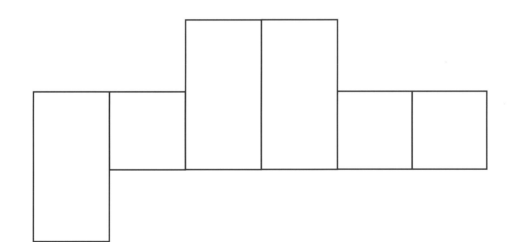

I5.2 Learning by sight

long vowels

PLURAL ENDINGS families *suffixes*

long vowels

SUFFIXES

prefixes handout

link words

1

2

3

4

5

6

7

8

9

10

11

12

Learning by sound

beginning
co-operative
impolite
telephone
interested
inconvenient
inextinguishable

---

d _ _ ry
rel _ _ nt
s _ _ _ _ _ quy
ac _ ident
g _ _ nt

Wednesday
Raspberry
Gnome
Knuckle
Parliament
Comb
Psychology

I7.1 Looking it up

1st
A-E

2nd
E-M

3rd
M-S

4th
S-Z

Section J: Vocabulary

J1.1 Working out the meaning of unfamiliar words

Antidisestablishmentarianism

Anti	dis	establish	ment	arian	ism
↓	↓	↓	↓	↓	↓
prefix	prefix	base word	suffix	suffix	suffix

Fascism which swept the continent earlier this century never gained a mass following in Britain. One reason is that antidisestablishmentarianism is a deep vein in British politics. The British have never liked change, and their instinct is to put down those who wish to overturn the power of church and state.

Quadrennial
Chronometer
Telethon
Exemplification

Terms of qualification

Only my coat was wet.

I like watching television, **mainly** sports programmes.

We **really** enjoyed your party.

The soup was **almost** too hot to eat.

J2.2 Terms of qualification

To subtract	
To be more specific or precise	
To heighten or emphasise	
To lower or limit	
To add or include	

1   All of us had saved up for a holiday except for James.

2   He visits regularly, mostly on Saturdays.

3   I fully agree with you.

4   I nearly missed you at the airport.

5   I really don't care.

6   She thought he was scarcely listening to her.

7   She was almost in tears.

8   Suzie has just finished her homework.

9   The journey was slightly uncomfortable.

10 They ate a huge meal and they also drank three bottles of wine.

11 They had travelled widely, mainly in Africa and India.

12 We want to pick the very best candidate for the job.

Terms of comparison

short   shorter   shortest

afraid	deep	tremendous	light
amazing	disgusting	hot	transparent
beautiful	dusty	important	lovely
cool	fair	interesting	narrow
silent	thin	serious	skinny
old	popular	pretty	reckless

J4.1 **Less or fewer?**

Mark ate _____ than Tom.

There are _____ boys than girls in the class.

Buy _____ butter.

Buy _____ apples.

I got _____ marks than you.

I get _____ pocket money than you.

There are _____ to go round.

There is _____ to go round.

Section K: Link words

K1.1 Connectives for comparing and contrasting

alternatively

otherwise

similarly

as with

instead of

equally

just as

likewise

unlike

like

in the same way

on the other hand

whereas

Words for comparing and contrasting

COMPARISON	CONTRAST
as with	alternatively
equally	instead of
in the same way	on the other hand
just as	otherwise
like	unlike
likewise	whereas
similarly	by contrast

K2.1 Temporal connectives

First of all …

Secondly,

Next….

When I had done that…

At the last moment…

Finally…

After	Next
At first	Now
At the last moment	Previously
At the same time	Once
Before	Since
During	Subsequently
First, second, third…	Then
Finally	Till
Following this	To begin with
Lastly	Until
Later	When
Meanwhile	Whereupon
	While
	Whilst

Causal connectives

a) Water expands as it freezes, so ice takes more space than water.

b) Sales are down because of high prices.

c) As a result of overnight rain, the pitch is not fit to use and therefore the match has been cancelled.

K3.2 Causal connectives

Words that link cause and effect

because

so that   resulting in

thus   the reason was

consequently

as a result

therefore

since   for

it follows that

as

naturally   so that

on account of

causing

as a consequence of

Connectives for adding and summating

Becoming a good cook has a number of advantages. Firstly, it improves your social life: everyone loves a good meal with great company, and everyone likes it when someone else does the cooking! It is also an opportunity to relax over a pastime that is appreciated by others. Furthermore there may be a career in it: you could become one of the rising number of celebrity television chefs!

There are, however, some important drawbacks. Think of the time spent preparing food and clearing up as well as waiting by the cooker. In addition, you should consider the time taken shopping for ingredients, and also the financial cost and plain hard work of serious cooking.

Chefs are agreed that, taking all the factors into consideration, the wise cook buys a dishwasher and also makes the family help with the preparation and clearing up. Overall, cooking has its drawbacks, but the results are worth it.

K4.2 Connectives for adding and summating

Connectives for adding and summing up

Adding

also

too

as well as

however

moreover

further

furthermore

Summating

in all

overall

all things considered

in the end

generally

as a rule

to sum up

Words for use in argument 1

Whereas	because	in conclusion
given that	so you see	this shows
assuming	therefore	nonetheless
considering	although	moreover
despite	in contrast	not only...but also
in short	while	furthermore
surely	it is clear that	consequently
on the other hand	nonetheless	obviously
certainly	whilst	clearly
and so	generally	overall
for example	for instance	as seen in
as shown by	as evidenced by	typified by
such as	indeed	absolutely
of course	naturally	undoubtedly

K6.1 Words for use in argument 2

Qualifying	Assuring	Cause & effect
Comparing	Contrasting	Summarising
Adding	Exemplifying	Emphasising

Creative thinking

What if people could fly?

Suppose we could read other people's minds.

Imagine you could live beneath water.

Maybe you will live forever.

What if we could speak every language in the world?

Perhaps you will marry someone you already know.

Questions	Conditionals	Instructions
What if...?	Maybe...	Imagine...

Section L: Language variation

L1.1 Words borrowed from other languages

menu
discotheque
abattoir

---

telephone

---

champagne
port
sherry
vodka

pizza
risotto
spaghetti
vermicelli
tortillas
fajitas
bhaji
crème fraiche
kebab

Words borrowed from other languages

List the borrowed word next to its country of origin:

didgeridoo	tea	igloo
movie	kindergarten	reggae
algebra	pyjamas	kimono
sherbet	kibbutz	bamboo
zero	balcony	chocolate
boomerang	carnival	caravan
motel	casino	matador
siesta	blitz	gondola

		Words
1.	America	
2.	America	
3.	Arabic	
4.	Arabic	
5.	Arabic	
6.	Australia	
7.	Australia	
8.	China	
9.	Eskimo	
10.	Germany	
11.	Germany	
12.	India	
13.	Israel	
14.	Italy	
15.	Italy	
16.	Italy	
17.	Italy	
18.	Jamaica	
19.	Japan	
20.	Malaya	
21.	Mexico	
22.	Persia	
23.	Spain	
24.	Spain	

L2.1 # Words with close relatives in other languages

German	bruder
Gaelic	bhrathair
Sanskrit	bhrata
Persian	biradar
English	_____

French	famille
German	familie
Latin	familia
English	_____

German	schule
Latin	schola
Greek	skhole
French	école
English	_____

French	femme
Latin	femina
English	_____

Latin	caballus
French	cheval
Spanish	caballo
Italian	cavallo
English	_____

202

American vocabulary and spelling

Color   humor   program

sidewalk   jelly

elevator   garbage

purse   firecrackers

gas   pants

frosting   fall

vest   ladybug

Hi!   cookies

zucchini   faucet

sweater   french fries

suspenders   thumb tack

candy   check

L4.1 Changing language

Faeder ure thu the eart on heofonum
si thin nama gehalgod

Our Father which art in heaven
Hallowed be thy name

Our Father in heaven
May your name be hallowed

Changing language

alien	tank top	wicked	virus	videotape
frock	yuppie	gay	cyberspace	luncheon
tights	separates	wireless	wrinklie	transistor
fanzine	search engines	trainers	lunar probe	commercial traveller
WORDS GOING OUT OF DATE	WORDS CHANGING IN MEANING	WORDS REFLECTING FASHION	WORDS RECENTLY INVENTED	WORDS REFLECTING NEW DISCOVERIES

L5.1 Meanings and context

love   over   penalty   round

A defined area on a computer screen in which part of a file or image can be displayed.

An opening in a wall to let in light and air, usually made of glass.

'We have lost our window of opportunity for launching the lunar probe because of poor weather conditions.'

force

source

energy

materials

Definitions

WORD: Test		
Word class	Meaning	Example of use

WORD: Beat		
Word class	Meaning	Example of use

WORD: Book		
Word class	Meaning	Example of use

WORD: Form		
Word class	Meaning	Example of use

WORD: Heat		
Word class	Meaning	Example of use